A Dog For All Seasons

Also by Jane E. Leon, D.V.M.

A Cat For All Seasons

Becoming Best Friends
(with Lisa D. Horowitz)

A Dog For All Seasons

Keeping Your Dog Healthy and Happy
Throughout the Year

Dr. Jane E. Leon, D.V.M.

Pecos Press
Tulsa, Oklahoma

Cover Design: Fuller, Dyal & Stamper, Inc.,

Interior Art Direction: Brooks-Clubb Production
          Project Manager: Barbara Brooks-Clubb
          Artists: Jim Dailey & Jic Clubb

Printed in the United States of America
10 9 8 7 6 5 4 3 2 1

To Melanie,
who has shown me the seasons
through the eyes of a child

Preface

There are numerous books devoted to the care of man's best friend, the dog. But this is the first book I know that addresses the dog's needs that crop up month after month, season after season. Once a puppy grows to adulthood, his immediate care is influenced more often by the temperature outdoors and the length of daylight rather than age, sex or any other factor.

I have spent more than ten years as a practicing veterinarian and five years dispensing advise as the author of "Pets and People," the syndicated pet care program on Associated Press Radio. During this time, I have discovered a pattern to people's concerns. Every year, the questions have to do less with basic care and more with seasonal issues. For example, I spend every spring discussing flea control and every winter explaining the dangers of poisonous holiday plants.

And so I wrote *A Dog For All Seasons*. This book points out the parts of your pet's care that vary in the spring, summer, fall and winter. Even though dogs are better adapted than we are to climate extremes, they still need our help to remain healthy. Your dog may wear his fur coat all year-round, yet he still needs a sweater in the winter and sunscreen in the summer.

Our dogs are part of our families. They share in our lives every day. I hope that *A Dog For All Seasons* will help make each day happy and rewarding for both your pet and you.

Jane E. Leon, D.V.M.
Wheaton, Maryland
December 1991

Contents

Part I

Spring

Chapter One
Spring Basics

As warm weather begins to chase away the cold, it is the perfect time to get your dog into shape. This is the time of year to chase away those winter blues and spruce up your dog's new spring coat. And if your pet has sat around the house all winter, he has probably lost muscle tone and gained weight. He will need to shed those excess pounds and start exercising. You can help him by putting him through spring training.

Spring Training

Spring training is an exercise program designed specifically for your dog. Dogs that exercise usually lead longer, healthier and happier lives. Physically, their body fat decreases and muscle mass increases. Their heart works more efficiently and their other body organs function better. Active dogs tend to have lower blood pressure and a smaller chance for heart disease than sedentary dogs. And they tend to lose weight. This results in joints, tendons and ligaments that feel and work better as well as a decreased incidence of arthritis.

Dogs that exercise also do better emotionally. They are less likely to use their energy to destroy the house and furnishings if they received adequate daily exercise. Dogs that get enough physical activity are happier, calmer and better able to handle any changes that may occur in their normal routine.

Just as you would see your physician before starting an exercise program, your dog's spring training starts with a visit to your veterinarian. Going to the clinic also gives your dog a chance to be tested for heartworm and get his annual vaccinations. These help keep him healthy during spring training and throughout the year.

Your veterinarian may have some good ideas about what exercises are best for your dog's particular condition. Young puppies and older dogs should not take part in strenuous activities that could result in injuries. The muscles, tendons, joints and bones of a puppy are not yet developed enough to withstand the stresses of rigorous, intensive training. If the animal is injured while he is still growing, he could end up with permanent physical disabilities.

Older dogs may have a condition that rules out heavy training. Excessive activity could exacerbate arthritis, redamage old injuries and create new ones in weakened joints, muscles and tendons. Gentle exercise is best for these animals and pets suffering from chronic injuries and ailments.

An overweight dog also requires special care. When an animal is carrying too much weight, his internal organs have to work harder and his blood pressure increases. When the dog is exercising, his organs and muscles need more oxygen and nutrients; the body may not be able to meet the demand. This can lead to overheating, organ failure and death. An overweight dog should not exercise strenuously. He should be put on a diet and regime of very mild exercise until his weight falls into the normal range. Then his activity level can be increased.

Once your dog has been cleared by your veterinarian, you can begin to design a program that suits his ability and needs. You can tell a great deal about how much activity your dog can handle by his breed and body build. Dogs that have long legs and a straight back line, such as greyhounds, whippets, salukis and wolfhounds, are good runners. Their center of gravity is often more towards the front legs than other breeds. Having been bred for speed, they enjoy running and chasing as they get their exercise.

Hounds and other hunting dogs are bred to track game over long distances. So, they would also enjoy running. Retrievers and dogs with large paws and strong legs are generally good swimmers. They like to fetch objects, both on land and in the water. Terriers and other dogs built close to the ground are designed for digging. They may enjoy vigorous activities such as fetch, catch or other activities that involve running over short distances. Lap dogs, such as the toy breeds, usually do not enjoy strenuous exercise. The extent of their running may be only through the house or in the backyard.

Walking Your Dog

One exercise that all dogs will benefit from is walking. It is the easiest activity and one of the best. A vigorous walk will give your dog many of the same health benefits as a jog or run, without the dangers. It accelerates the heart rate but does not place undue stress on the ligaments and tendons. It also reduces the chance of stress fractures in young and old bones. Walking is also an excellent exercise for debilitated pets, such as those with heart disease or joint disease.

A walking program should begin with a slow, 15-minute walk. If your pet is not winded after returning home, you can pick up the pace and increase the distance the next day. You can also increase the number of walks. The goal is to have him walk for a fairly good distance at a fast and steady gait. You do not want to set a pace that allows frequent stops to check out the surroundings. With the exception of stopping for rest and water whenever necessary, your dog should keep moving.

Make sure that you do not overextend your dog. It is all right if your pet gets fatigued, but he should not become exhausted or collapse. He may want to flop down after returning home but he should be getting up within a few minutes. He should be able to move about easily if he needs to and he should always be alert. And he should be interested in going back outside, if he gets the chance. If he would rather lie and watch you leave, in all likelihood, he has overexerted himself. You should cut back on his exercise a little until his stamina increases.

A common problem among urban dogs is that they often get brief walks during the week and then have extended exercise periods on the weekend. This can lead to an injury-prone dog. The ligaments and tendons simply cannot handle the stress of infrequent heavy exercise. As a result, the animal can suffer strains and sprains. Just because your dog has four legs does not mean that he is always ready for strenuous exercise. If you are not in condition for a strenuous exercise session, in all likelihood, neither is your dog. You can improve his conditioning for the weekend by giving him longer periods of exercise and play during the week. Perhaps you can take him out two or three times a day rather than just one.

Jogging With Your Dog

You also must prepare your dog to be your jogging companion. A dog that is out of shape can suffer the same sorts of injuries from jogging that a person can. Dogs can develop knee, elbow and hip problems, as well as the usual sprains and strains. Treatment for the injuries can range from simple rest to surgery.

And just like a person, a dog should gradually build up in strength before embarking on a running program. It can often take a person four to five weeks to get in shape for jogging. A dog needs the same amount of time. Your dog can follow the same program that you do. Since even small amounts of exercise are good, there is no need to rush into a rigorous program.

Before starting out on a jog, you undoubtedly warm up. Your dog should, too. A few minutes of light play in the yard will help loosen up his joints, stretch out his muscles and get his heart beating faster. If he is warmed up when he begins to run, the chance of injury will be reduced.

Your dog and you should run on dirt or grass

whenever possible. Because these surfaces are softer than asphalt and concrete, the amount of stress on the legs is reduced. Plus, you should keep an eye out for holes, cracks, stumps and other obstacles that can trip your pet. A dog in motion does not always look where he is going. After a period of heavy activity, both your jogging companion and you should warm down. Walking for a short distance will help prevent the muscles from tightening up.

Precautions To Observe

One exercise that is not good for your dog is running him while you ride a bicycle. If your dog is not on a leash, you will not be able to control him. If he is, he can easily become tangled up in it. This may cause him to choke and you to fall over. Even if he does manage to run alongside, a slow pace for you on a bike may be too fast for your dog. Because he is tethered by the leash, he is forced to keep up. He can become overexerted.

In addition, you should be cautious about exercising as the weather becomes progressively warmer. Avoid walking or jogging during the hottest times of the day. Hot pavement can burn your dog's feet. More importantly, your dog will overheat faster than you do. Strenuous exercise can lead to heatstroke. Whenever exercising, you should allow your dog to rest and drink water every twenty to thirty minutes. If you notice that your dog is drooling and panting more than usual, stop for additional rest and water. And then, take him home; he has had enough.

One last precaution needs to be mentioned. While exercising, you should keep your dog on a leash unless you are in a fenced area. Even if your dog is well-trained and has never left your side, the temptation to chase a squirrel, cat or another dog may be too much to resist. One slip-up can end in tragedy. A dog that darts out into the street can be hit by a car. Using a leash will keep your dog safe.

Dieting

During the winter, your dog may have put on some weight. During cold weather, pets tend to eat more and exercise less. This is important for outdoor dogs because they need the excess calories to keep warm. But other pets simply end up with an extra layer of wintertime fat. So, when spring arrives, your dog may be overweight.

There are a number of problems caused by being overweight. If your dog is obese, he is not healthy. As a matter of fact, the excess weight is so bad for him that the condition could be considered a disease. An obese dog has difficulty rising, walking, running and lying down. His body organs, including his heart, lungs, liver and kidneys, are constantly stressed as they attempt to manage a body burdened by excess fat. And his ligaments, joints, tendons and bones suffer from excessive wear and tear, resulting in arthritis and lameness. The severity of the physical problems tends to increase with age. Overweight dogs often lead shorter, less comfortable lives than dogs kept at their proper weight.

As previously mentioned, an overweight dog should not undertake any strenuous exercise. It could overtax his already stressed organ system, exacerbating medical problems. The excess weight can contribute to arthritis and degenerative conditions effecting discs, ligaments and tendons; heavy activity could worsen these conditions and cause pain.

Overweight dogs also tend to develop fatty tumors. These growths are usually benign but they can cause discomfort. The fatty lumps grow under the skin in many different areas of the body. If they grow under the tail, they interfere with tail motion. If they grow beneath an armpit, they can hinder walking. Because they can affect your dog's range of motion and make him uncomfortable, the tumors often require surgical removal. Keeping your dog at his proper weight may reduce the incidence of these growths.

There are a couple of ways to check to see if your dog needs to lose a few pounds. The first is by using your sight. When your dog is standing, look at him from the side. You should be able to notice good definition between the rib cage and the abdominal area. If you cannot tell where the ribs end and the abdomen begins, your dog is overweight.

Another method uses your sense of touch. While the dog is standing, place your hands on both sides of the rib cage. If you can just barely feel the ribs, your dog is within range of his optimum weight. If you can put your fingers between the ribs, your dog is too thin. However, if you cannot feel the ribs at all, the animal should go on a diet.

Just as for people who are dieting, safety is the most important consideration. The first step is to consult your veterinarian. Your doctor can determine your dog's ideal weight and then outline a plan to reach that goal safely over a period of weeks. For smaller dogs, the target is to lose about one-half pound of weight per week; larger dogs should lose about one pound a week.

After checking with your veterinarian, you should spend a day or two documenting everything that your dog eats. The results may surprise you. Pets generally eat much more than you think. When you have compiled that information, you can decide how to proceed.

There are a couple of things to remember. First, while you will be feeding your dog less, he still needs a balanced diet. The food that he eats should contain proper levels of protein, fat and carbohydrates.

Second, a dog should not be starved to lose weight. Weight loss should be gradual over an extended period of time. An animal needs a certain amount of calories to feel well and do well every day.

If he does not get them, his body will begin to burn its own tissue to survive. That is very bad. And it frequently results in weight loss that cannot be maintained over a period of time. As soon as the dog starts to eat again, he gains back all of the weight and more.

Third, regardless of what sort of diet method is used, your dog must have access to a constant source of fresh water. It is a crucial component of a balanced diet. An animal can survive much longer without food than he can without water.

In most cases, you will have to make some sort of adjustment in the amount of food that your dog eats. One obvious method is to eliminate most snacks and treats. This applies especially to tablescraps. They often contain a great deal of fat and quite a few calories. Giving your dog fewer biscuits will also reduce his daily intake without cutting back on his meals.

A second method is to reduce the amount fed for his regular meals. As a rule of thumb, you can safely decrease your dog's diet by about 20 to 30 percent. So, if you normally feed your dog three cups of food, you should reduce that amount to around two and a half cups. If your dog has trouble adjusting to eating less, you may be able to help him curb his appetite. Try feeding him several smaller meals rather than one or two big meals. This might satisfy your dog as he becomes hungry throughout the day. It is important, however, that you increase only the number of meals. The total amount of food given in a 24-hour period should be consistent with the diet plan.

A third possibility is to change the type of food.

Today, there are several good "lite" foods available. These are composed of the same nutrients and flavors as regular food except that they have more non-digestible fillers. Because of these fillers, the animal gets less calories in each mouthful. By changing to one of these foods, you might be able to feed your dog the same amount and still achieve the needed calorie reduction for a safe diet. The only problem is that, because these foods contain so much undigestible matter, your dog will produce larger stools. Many get gas, as well.

While your dog is dieting, you should make sure that he remains healthy. He should be alert, responsive and energetic. In addition, his eyes should shine and his coat should be rich and glossy. If not, he may be having problems. You should then contact your veterinarian for advice.

Also, measure your dog's progress every week. You might even want to keep a chart to document his headway. If, after four weeks or so, your pet has not lost any weight, you should investigate his activities. The dog might be so hungry that he is constantly begging. And everyone in the family, feeling sorry for him, might be slipping the animal small tidbits of food throughout the day. One or two small tidbits per each family member add up to a dog who is not really on a diet. In order for the diet to be successful, extraneous snacks must be curbed.

Besides decreasing the number of calories going in, you should increase the number of calories being burned off. This can be done with exercise. As discussed earlier, the introduction of exercise should be slow and easy. Short walks are best. The duration of the walks can be gradually increased as the dog's condition improves. The added exercise and attention will keep your dog's mind off of food and help burn extra calories.

Once your pet has reached his ideal weight, you can start to increase the amount of food that he eats. But he should not go back to his normal eating pattern. That was what made him overweight. And you cannot rely on the directions on the food package labels; they are only guidelines. You will have to balance the quantity of food and treats fed against the dog's exercise level and lifestyle. Over a short period of time, you should be able to determine the combination that will provide your dog with a balanced diet and maintain his proper weight.

Shedding

As the weather warms up, you might notice that your dog is shedding more. The logical explanation is that he is losing his winter coat. The dog's coat will naturally adjust itself in order for the animal to be more comfortable during the warmer seasons. But that is not the whole story.

The coat does adjust for the seasons. During the colder months, the hair is usually finer and thinner. This allows it to lie down next to other hairs in a tight-knit fashion. It can then insulate the dog against the cold. The interlocking effect will keep the cold air from reaching the animal's skin and reflect the dog's own body heat back on him. Some breeds have a double coat; the undercoat is composed of hair that is finer and more tightly situated.

During the warmer months, however, the hairs are coarser. They cannot lie as closely together. This opens the coat more, increasing the circulation of air on the skin while continuing to block the sun's rays. All this helps keep the dog cool.

Since there are two types of coats, there are usually two main sheds per year. In the spring, your dog lose his fine winter coat and replace it with his coarse summer coat. Surprisingly, shedding seems to have more to do with the change in light than in temperature. This explains why all dogs shed, no matter what sort of climate they live in. It is the longer days, not the warmth, that set the spring shed in motion. The same holds true in the fall. When the days become shorter, the animal will lose his summer hair and begin growing his winter coat.

The two major sheds are not the only ones, however. For most dogs, shedding is an everyday occurrence. The life cycle of an animal's hair is straightforward. A hair grows, sits for a period of time and then falls out. This makes room for the growth of a new hair. If this happened all at once, your pet would completely shed his coat and grow a new one every so often. But it does not work that way. At any given moment, some hairs are growing, some are sitting and some are falling out. So, your pet sheds year-round.

Even dogs that supposedly do not shed actually do lose hair. Breeds such as poodles, schnauzers and terriers are often the pet of choice for people with allergies. The theory is that these animals do not shed. In fact, they do. But the hair tends to stick to the coat and form mats instead of falling out all over the house. And that is why these animals need to be professionally groomed every four to six weeks. The dead hair has to be removed.

At some time during the year, you may be concerned that your dog is losing too much hair. It is true that illness and stress can affect your pet's coat. And hair that has matted together will often come out in clumps. However, there is an easy way to determine if the amount is too much. If the hair loss results in very thin patches of hair or bare spots, then the amount is excessive. On the other hand, if the animal remains completely covered with hair, then there is nothing to be concerned about. In most cases, the dog is not losing hair in clumps; the dead hair has simply matted together and is falling out all at once.

The best way to handle constant shedding is to brush your dog every day. This will allow you to remove most of the dead hair in one place, keeping it from being spread all over the house. Regular grooming will also give you a chance to examine your pet's hair and skin so you can determine if excessive shedding is occurring. And it helps keep your dog's coat healthy, enabling it to performing its seasonal function of protecting and insulating the animal.

Daily brushing also prevents the dead hair from forming large, dense mats. These need to be avoided for a couple of reasons. First, they create areas underneath them that are shielded from sun and air. These areas are perfect hiding places for parasites such as fleas and ticks. Second, the skin under the mats tends to be irritated and moist, creating an environment conducive to inflammation and infection.

Bathing Your Dog

A dog rarely needs a bath. You should not give him one unless there is a very good reason for it. His hair has natural oils that protect his coat and skin. In most cases, your dog can be kept reasonably clean with regular brushing.

However, there comes a time when every dog needs a bath. His coat may be very dirty or giving off a bad odor. He may be infested with fleas. Or he might have a skin condition or another medical reason that calls for a bath. You may find it easier to delegate this task to your veterinarian or a professional groomer. But if there is no one else available, you will have to do it yourself.

There is a proper way to bathe your dog. First, you should remove any mats that may be in his coat. If not, they will interfere with the hair being dried. In addition, the hair around the mats will clump into them when wet, creating even bigger mats. If you cannot comb or brush the mats out, you will have to clip them.

Next, select a shampoo that is made for dogs. Shampoos for humans are not good; the pH is often wrong. Some people use mild dishwashing soap on their pets. But it can strips the oils out of the coat, resulting in dry, flaky, itchy skin. This can lead to excessive scratching, which in turn leads to infection.

For whatever reason your dog needs a bath, you should be able to find a shampoo that suits him. If your pet has very dry skin, you may want to purchase a conditioner, as well. If you just want to clean the animal, use shampoo that is very neutral and mild. As you choose the shampoo, read the directions carefully. Different shampoos call for different precautions.

Then, take steps to protect the dog's sensitive areas from the soap and water. Put a piece of cotton in each ear to keep water out. A drop of an ocular lubricant or mineral oil in both eyes will protect them from soap.

If your dog will be bathed in a tub, place a rubber mat on the bottom to prevent slips and falls. This may make the dog feel more secure. Keeping your dog from becoming nervous may help prevent the bath from becoming one of the great misadventures of your life.

After completing the precautionary steps, you are ready to begin. Thoroughly wet the entire dog. Dogs are easier to bathe if you use a sprayer with a nozzle and let the water drain as you give the bath. Most do not like being dumped into a tub full of standing water. It is a good idea to keep one hand on the animal at all times. This will help steady and possibly calm him.

Apply the shampoo according to the directions. You probably should put some shampoo into your hand and then rub it on your dog. This will allow you to obtain a more even application. Pouring the substance directly on your pet may result in too large a concentration in a small area. This is difficult to rinse out and might irritate the dog's skin.

Start by cleaning the head. In this area, the shampoo must be applied by your hands or with a cloth. Even though you took steps to prevent irritation, do your best to keep the soap out of the eyes and ears. If it is not needed, avoid putting soap on the face altogether. Then work your way along the back and sides towards the tail. The legs should be cleaned last.

Then comes the most important part of the bath: the rinse. The entire dog must be rinsed until every trace of soap is gone. Any left on the animal will dry and irritate the skin. Use plenty of fresh water. The head should be held up so that the water will drain down the neck rather than onto the face. Keep the ear covered by the ear flap.

After the bath, vigorously towel dry your pet. This will massage and stimulate the skin. Or you can use a hair dryer set very low. Make sure that the animal is kept warm until completely dry. A wet dog chills easily. After your pet is dry, thoroughly brush the dog to prevent any tangles from forming.

Pet Insurance

As your dog becomes more active in the spring, the chance that he will have an accident and be injured increases. An accident can happen at any time and place. Veterinary medicine has advanced to the point that, even with a very serious injury, your pet will have a good chance of survival. Unfortunately, some of these lifesaving procedures are also very expensive. Too often, a person is caught between authorizing a costly procedure or saying goodbye to a beloved companion.

An insurance policy for your dog would eliminate that horrible predicament. A policy for your dog works just like a policy for you. You select a policy with the coverage that you want and pay a yearly premium based on the type of plan and your pet's age. For each veterinary visit, you pay a deductible and the insurance company pays the rest of the bill. While the number of companies that offer insurance now are few, the availability of this type of service is slowly expanding.

In some areas, Health Maintenance Organizations, called HMO's, exist. These are designed just like the preventative medical plans for people. With a plan such as this, you pay only a set amount each year for medical care. After that point, the rest of your expenses are covered by your insurance.

Pet insurance sounds great, but it may not be for everyone. The rates and services vary widely among the few companies that carry these policies. You need to read the contract carefully and consider the cost-effectiveness for your own situation. Most plans do not cover routine care, vaccinations or elective surgeries. They also exclude older animals from illness insurance, limiting payments to injuries only.

If you are considering pet insurance, talk to your veterinarian. The doctor can give you the names and details of plans in your area. And you just might find out that your clinic has its own plan.

Chapter Two
In the Yard

Since your dog will be spending more time outside in the spring, your yard deserves a walk-through. You should take a look around both your front and back yards to see what potential mischief your dog can get into. This evaluation of your yard should not take much time. All that you need to do is check to see that it is a safe and hazard-free environment.

On the Lawn

A general rule of thumb to follow is that, with the exception of the sun and water, everything that is good for your lawn is bad for your dog. The products that you use on your lawn to make the grass and shrubs look great are all potentially poisonous to animals. These include herbicides, fertilizers and insecticides. And ingesting the treated grass is not the only way that your dog can become sick; he can become poisoned just from walking on it. When taking a stroll across your lawn, your dog may get some fertilizer or weed killer on his feet. If the chemicals start to irritate your pet, he will probably lick them off. This can lead to medical problems, including digestive disorders, kidney failure and liver disease.

The labels on most lawn and garden products will advise you how to use them safely. But observing a few extra precautions is a good idea. It is best for the environment and your pet if you use lawn and garden products only where they are needed. Perhaps only the grass beneath trees or around shrubs needs the aid of chemicals to be full and lush. Or the lawn is in good shape but the garden requires additives. If you can avoid covering the entire yard, you will reduce the exposure of your dog to these harsh chemicals.

A second precaution is to keep your pet off of any treated area for at least a day. During that time, you should follow the fertilizer manufacturer's recommended steps for soaking the additive into the soil. In many cases, this is a thorough watering. Some weed and insect killers need to be left on the grass for 24 hours before you can water the lawn. In a case such as that, your dog will need to be confined for two days. The microencapsulated products that break down over several weeks usually are not practical for the yard of a pet owner.

Another good idea is to erect barriers that will keep your dog off of the treated areas. For a garden or small sections of your lawn, you may be able to use netting or chicken wire to deny access to your dog. If you cover the whole yard with chemicals, you may want to keep the dog indoors or on a leash whenever you take him out.

A further precaution is to clean your dog's feet after he walks on any treated areas. Even a thorough watering after application will not remove all traces of fertilizer or other lawn products. But if you rinse and wipe his feet after your dog gets on the grass, you will be able to remove any potentially dangerous substance before the animal can be harmed by it. If you own a very short dog and have tall grass, you should wipe off his chest and abdomen as well as his feet.

One last precaution is to not allow your dog to roam freely around the neighborhood. You may use fertilizers and weed killers that are mild and non-toxic for animals, but you cannot count on your neighbors to do so, as well. Quite reasonably, the other people on your block will use the products that best suit their needs. So,while your yard will be safe for your pet, the yards next door and down the street may not be. All of your exhaustive efforts to protect your dog will go for naught if he accidentally poisons himself in another yard on the block.

Other items in the yard besides chemicals can be toxic. Many plants, shrubs and tree leaves can be very harmful to an animal if ingested. The number and types of poisonous plants vary from location to location; the most common are the rhododendron, mountain laurel, lily, azalea, black locust, cherry tree and oak tree. A good rule to follow is that a plant should be considered toxic unless you know for certain that it is not. Even if the plant is not harmful, you should be wary of its seeds or bulbs. These are generally coated with insecticide and antifungal agents. You should try to keep your dog from digging in areas where seeds and bulbs are planted.

Even non-toxic plants can be hazardous. The seeds of some plants and grasses are very sharp. They can stick in the hair, penetrate the skin or lodge in an ear. This causes a local inflammatory reaction and infection that can require surgery to treat. You should check your dog daily and remove burrs, thorns, seeds and other plant matter from his coat before it can cause trouble.

In the Garage

Besides working in the yard during the spring, you may be sprucing up the exterior of your house. Items like paints, turpentine and sealants are often stored in the garage. And there is usually sweet-tasting coolant for the car as well as gasoline and oil for the lawn mower. If you have a swimming pool, there may be pool cleaners and chemicals lying about. Most of these products are very toxic or even deadly for an animal. You should take all the necessary precautions to see that your dog does not get into them.

Animals do not have enough sense to stay away from foul-tasting substances. They often get into and ingest a product before making a determination that it does not taste good. There have been cases where dogs have chewed through plastic bottles of detergent bleach just because they liked the way the plastic felt while chewing it. And they continued to chew without any regard to the fact that their mouths were being burned. This sort of behavior is more often found in puppies than adult dogs.

When it comes to working with and storing poisonous products, you should treat your pet as you would your child. You should keep your pet away from open containers of paint and other chemicals when you are using them. When putting a product away, place it on a shelf at a height that an animal cannot reach or jump to. In addition, all chemicals and solvents should be stored in their original containers. That way, if your pet should accidentally get into a toxic or burning chemical, you will be able to identify the product. Knowing what caused the problem may help in determining how to treat it. If you do change containers, make sure that they are properly labeled. They should also be sealed tightly. If you notice any corrosion or leaks in a container, throw it away.

Signs of a Poisoned Dog and What To Do

Most cases of poisoning are self-induced. You probably will not see your dog poison himself. You might suspect it, however, if you notice that he is acting in a abnormal manner. For example, many people believe that a dog will eat grass after swallowing a poisonous or nondigestable substance. The theory is that ingesting the grass will cause the dog to regurgitate the grass as well as everything else in the stomach. This may be true. However, many perfectly healthy dogs graze consistently.

What you should watch for is a change in behavior. So, if your dog has a habit of munching on the lawn, you should not be concerned. However, if your dog has never eaten grass but then suddenly starts to do so, you should assume that something is wrong.

In addition, he may show signs of illness that merit a trip to your veterinarian. Different poisons can cause different sympotms. Most often, they are gastrointestinal, respiratory and neurological dysfunctions. They include vomiting, diarrhea, shaking, convulsions, excessive drooling and difficulty breathing. Other signs include weakness, collapse, irritated eyes and mouth, evidence of a peculiar substance on the coat and blood in vomit, feces or urine.

If you notice any of these signs, you should contact your veterinarian immediately for advise. If you cannot reach your veterinarian, call the local poison control center. Most likely, you will need to take your dog to the clinic for emergency treatment. But there are a few common-sense steps that might help reduce the effect of the poison. First of all, if the poison is on the skin, you should wash it off using a lot of water. (Be sure to wear gloves to reduce the chance of poisoning yourself.) You should also try to get your dog to drink as much water as possible. Most poisons will be diluted by water. Then you should go to your veterinarian as soon as possible.

There are also a couple of things that you should not do. First of all, if you should happen to see your dog ingest or come in contact with a toxic substance, do not wait until the signs of being poisoned develop. Instead, take him to the veterinarian at once. Also do not induce vomiting unless you are instructed to do so by your veterinarian. Many poisons burn. The throat was burned once as the poison went down; bringing the toxin back up might burn it again.

At the veterinary clinic, the doctor will probably treat your pet's symptoms. There are limited antidotes for poisons. Even if you know exactly what your dog swallowed, an antidote will usually not have much effect once the animal starts showing symptoms. Your veterinarian may try some steps to reduce the amount of poison in the body. One is to give medicinal charcoal tablets or liquid; these will absorb many toxins. Another is to induce vomiting. In most cases, however, the best treatment is supportive care. The animal is given copious and continuous amounts of fluid, vitamins and electrolytes. These are administered until the poison is eliminated and its effects have worn off.

Other Hazards In the Yard

Besides poisons, your yard presents other hazards that can affect your dog. Your fence may have holes in it that you did not notice while spending the winter indoors. There may be big, muddy spots that can make the dog filthy, which can lead to skin irritations. An outdoor wooden deck may have suffered the effects of months of harsh weather; your dog might get splinters from it. Or there may be areas of standing, stagnant water that are breeding grounds for mosquitos and other biting insects. Most of these hazards can be eliminated with minor efforts and repairs.

In addition, this is the season when the parasitic worm eggs that were dormant all winter become infective. If you did not do so on a regular basis during the winter, you should now clean up all of the dog feces in your yard. Even if your dog has been clear of intestinal worms, other dogs that have them may have left droppings in various spots.

Spring is also a good time to check your yard for poison ivy, poison oak and poison sumac. These plants can be the cause of allergic skin reactions. The plant oils, if they touch the skin of susceptible individuals, can lead to itchy rashes.

There is good and bad news concerning this group of hazardous plants. The good news is that your dog will probably never suffer from the skin rashes caused by these plants. The irritating oils rarely penetrate your dog's top coat and get down to the skin.

The bad news is that while the irritating oils do not penetrate the coat, they will remain on it. So, if you give your dog a big hug after he has run through a patch of poison ivy, you may soon have a severe case of poison ivy allergic dermatitis. Even though your dog probably will not suffer from exposure to these plants, it is best for everyone if these plants do not grow in your yard. If you have to remove them, be sure to wear to gloves. And do not burn them; the burning oils can cause allergic reactions in the mouth, eyes and other parts of the body.

Chapter Three
Fleas

After coming back inside from one of his spring romps, your dog may start to scratch excessively. If that happens, it is almost a guarantee that your pet did not come inside alone. He probably brought fleas with him. And you will have to act fast to head off the problems caused by your unwelcome guests.

What Are Fleas?

Fleas are the most common external parasites found on both cats and dogs. They are small, brown-black, wingless insects that feed on the blood of mammals. In warmer climates, they are a year-round problem. In most, however, they make their appearance as the weather warms and the humidity increases. The ideal conditions would be a temperature between 65 and 80 degrees with the humidity at 75 percent or higher.

Fleas can be virtually anywhere outside. They often live in tall grass, bushes and gardens. As an unsuspecting dog wanders by, the fleas jump on. Once aboard, they often migrate to areas that the animal cannot reach very well. These include the base of the tail, under the belly line, the back of the legs and around the ears and neck. In an effort to get rid of these pests, your dog will continuously scratch and bite himself.

Unfortunately, fleas are very hard to catch. They have laterally compressed bodies; they are long and thin. This allows them to move easily through your pet's dense coat. They also have long legs, making them very quick and exceptional jumpers. At any given time, a flea can jump up to three feet. That is equivalent to a six-foot man jumping over the Washington Monument.

Besides your dog biting and scratching, you might see other signs of a flea problem. One is flea dirt on your dog's hair and skin. These grainy, black specks of dirt are, in reality, flea excrement. Since fleas feed on your pet's blood, flea excrement is comprised primarily of dried blood. In fact, if you wet it, it produces a deep red stain.

Another sign is a flea itself. If your pet has pale hair or lightly pigmented skin, you might actually see one on the animal. The best spots to look are those areas where the coat is the thinnest, such as the abdomen and underarms.

If you find one or two fleas, you might think that the problem is so small that it can be ignored. But even one flea can make your pet and you miserable in a very short period of time. After feeding on your dog, a flea will start to lay eggs. If the conditions are optimal, one flea can lay well over 400 eggs in her lifetime. The eggs will roll off of your dog and can lodge virtually anywhere in your house. They will hatch in about a week. It can take only three weeks for the flea larvae to develop into egg-laying adults themselves. So, within just one month, that one flea and its offspring can number in the thousands.

If the existing conditions are not right for development, the eggs can lie dormant for months, waiting for a better time to hatch. The larvae can also wait for the ideal conditions before maturing into adults. Once they do, these fleas can feed on any resident of your household. This includes the dog, the cat and every other member of your family.

The Dangers of Fleas

At best, a single flea bite will result only in a mild reaction in your dog. One flea, sucking out a small quantity of blood, will cause your pet to scratch or bite at the spot every so often but show few other signs of discomfort. However, it is very rare that your dog will have just one flea. A large population can draw enough blood to result in a low red cell count and anemia. The effect is often general fatigue and an intolerance to exercise. It also makes the animal more susceptible to infection and can lead to organ failure. There have been cases where puppies have died of blood loss.

Fleas also spread diseases. When they bite through the skin to feed on the blood, the parasites can transmit germs and other disease-causing organisms.

They have been shown to infect cats with the plague.

In addition, they are a major conduit of tapeworm infections. Tapeworms are common intestinal parasites found in dogs. Immature fleas feed on tapeworm eggs. In the process of trying to rid himself of fleas, a dog may swallow a flea that has a developing tapeworm inside. The tapeworm continues to mature and goes on to infect the animal. Untreated, tapeworms can cause diarrhea and weight loss. Even though these parasites are easy to kill with medicine, it is very hard to eliminate a tapeworm problem entirely. Every time your dog swallows a flea, he stands a good chance of reinfection.

Another problem is that many dogs are allergic to fleas. In fact, fleas are the number one cause of allergic reactions in canines. For a dog that is hypersensitive, a single flea bite can mean a severe skin reaction with itching, rashes, sores and hair loss. A reaction can take several days to run its course.

In some instances, a dog becomes so itchy that he will tear out his fur and actually bite himself until he creates open sores. Because the sores are painful, the animal continues to bite and lick the spot. This can lead to a skin infection. The moist, infected area is known as a hot spot; it requires veterinary treatment. If untreated, a hot spot can become very large in a short period of time.

In a household with more than one pet, often one will have a worse problem with fleas than the other. The same holds true for people. While fleas can bite any person, some seem more prone to getting them than others. And the sensitivity to the bite varies among people as it does animals. So, one flea poses a threat to the health of your entire family.

Flea Control

Flea control is difficult. The problem stems from the fact that fleas do not live just on your dog; they infiltrate your house and yard, as well. You cannot just give your pet a flea bath and expect the problem to be gone. A flea bath will kill the fleas that are on your dog but will do nothing about the rest of the fleas in his environment. Your pet may be flea-free for a few hours, but he will be subject to further infestation as soon as he goes back outside or lies down in his bed.

To attack the flea population adequately, you must have a strategy. As you formulate your battle plan, you need to keep a few things in mind. The treatment of your dog and his environment must be simultaneous. You will not be successful treating your pet one day, treating the house the next and doing the yard the day after that. By the time that you get around to treating the yard, reinforcements will have already spread back into your house and onto your dog. Treating all three on the same day will put a dent in the flea population and should keep the parasites off of your pet for several days, if not weeks.

A balanced approach is also safer for your dog. Most items used to kill fleas are insecticides; in other words, they are poisons. By treating his environment, you will reduce the number of fleas that jump on your dog. This, in turn, means that you can limit the amount of toxic chemicals applied directly to his body.

In addition, you need to make sure that the products that you use are compatible. It is possible that the insecticide for the yard should not be used in conjunction with the one for the house or the dog. The wrong combination of products may make your pet sick. It can also be hazardous to the other members of your family. Most products will have information about what other chemicals can be used with them. Before buying any insecticide, you should read all of the information on the label and packaging. This will ensure that the product will suit your particular needs and be safe to use.

Treating Your Yard

Most insecticides designed for outside use have two components. The first is a chemical that kills all of the adult fleas present. The second is a growth regulator designed to prevent the larvae from maturing into egg-laying adults. This residual compound is often microencapsulated; it sinks into the ground and becomes active over the course of days, weeks or months. The literature that comes with the product will give the length of time that the chemical will be potent and exact directions as to use and toxicity. It will also list warnings so as to ensure the safety of all of the people, animals and plants in the area.

Besides following all of the product's instructions, there are a few steps that you can take to make flea control safer and more effective. First, you should keep the yard as clean as possible. This is accomplished by frequnetly cutting the grass short, getting rid of dead shrubs and trimming bushes back. This reduces the amount of moisture held in the vegetation. A drier environment is less conducive to flea reproduction. Also, it keeps the yard less cluttered and more exposed to sunlight. These help keep the flea population down, as well.

Second, you should treat your entire yard, not just the areas frequented by your dog. Even though your dog is confined to the backyard, fleas in the front may be able to get to him. They may hitch a ride to the back on your clothing or shoes. Or they may come inside the house and jump on him there. The goal is to create a barrier that fleas will not be able to penetrate. The wider the perimeter of the barrier, the less likely that the fleas will be able to reach your pet.

Treating Your House

Just like their outdoor counterparts, indoor insecticides usually have two components: a quick-kill stage and a residual. Flea products designed for in-house use are usually sprays or foggers. Sprays focus the application of the insecticide. This enables you to reach into cracks and crevices of walls, carpets and closets. Foggers are aerosolized chemicals whose mist evenly covers a wide area in a short period of time. When treating your house, a combination of the two products is usually needed.

Using two products in your house at the same time means that you should take extra care to select compatible products and follow their instructions closely. And, just as when treating your yard, you can take steps to make treating your house safer and more effective.

One of the best steps is to clean and vacuum your house thoroughly before treating it. This will remove some of the fleas that hide in the carpets and furniture. Steam cleaning the carpets can help if you get the water very hot. You should also either wash your dog's bedding in hot water or replace it.

Next, you should cut off airflow systems while the house is being treated. If not, the chemicals can get sucked into the central air conditioning ducts, reducing the concentration of the insecticide before the mist has a chance to work. It also prevents the continued circulation of the insecticides when the system is on. Breathing the chemicals could make everyone in your household sick.

Third, the house should be vacant for a few hours after it is treated. This gives the insecticide time to work. It also keeps your pet and you from inhaling an excess amount of the product. You might want to drop your dog off at the groomer's or your veterinary clinic for the day. And you should stay away for the prescribed amount of time, as well.

Last, watch for hypersensitive reactions to the chemicals. Even after the insecticide has settled and dried, it leaves an odor and a residual component. It is possible that your pet or another family member may be allergic to the product. If there is a problem, you will have to clean the house thoroughly again. On that occasion, you will be doing so to remove the insecticide, not the fleas that it killed.

Treating Your Dog

Once the yard and house have been treated, you should treat your dog. It seems like there are more flea products available than there are fleas. The variety of products is so extensive that it is hard to know which ones to use. Which flea products are best for you depend on several factors. These include the severity of the flea problem as well as the type and temperament of your pet. While an indoor dog may need only a flea collar, a large outdoor dog usually needs a much more rigorous approach to flea control.

Most flea products can be divided into two categories: insecticides and repellents. Insecticides are the most effective tools for controlling fleas. They kill all of the fleas that are on your pet; many have a residual effect that takes care of new fleas for a period of time.

However, insecticides do have some drawbacks. Being poisons, they can make your dog sick. This is usually the result of using too much of a product or using more than one product at a time. They also have a limited residual period, often requiring frequent applications. This increases your dog's exposure to the chemicals. In addition, insecticides have a cumulative effect. Over a period of time, the amount of the toxins in your dog's system will build up. Thus, a dose that was initially safe may make your pet sick if used repeatedly for five or six weeks.

When using an insecticide, you can take a few steps to insure your pet's continued good health. First, you should consult with your veterinarian before starting any flea eradication program. The doctor has access to the latest information on various products and their safety. She can also outline any special precautions that need to be followed for your dog. In addition, puppies, older pets and dogs that are sick or injured should not be exposed to flea products without veterinary supervision.

Second, always read and follow all of the manufacturer's directions. Be sure that the product is made specifically for dogs. Most will inform you how to safely use that product and list other insecticides that can be used with it. You can employ multiple products, but you might have to limit their use. For example, you may need to leave a flea collar off of your dog for a week after treating him with a flea dip.

Third, test the product before using it on a full-scale basis. One way to do this is to watch for an adverse reaction after putting a small amount of the insecticide on your pet. Start out by applying the product to one-third of the animal's body. You should then keep an eye on the dog for the next 24-hours, watching for any unusual symptoms or behavior. If your dog does not show any signs of trouble, you can then feel safe about using the product on his entire body. However, if there is a problem, use plain water to rinse off the flea product and take the animal to your veterinarian.

This section is not meant to discourage the use

of insecticides; adequate flea control is nearly impossible without them. They are good, safe products as long as you use them carefully and with restraint. The most common insecticide products are flea collars, powders, sprays, shampoos and dips.

Flea Collars

One of the most common and inexpensive flea products is the flea collar. However, there is some controversy over just how effective it is. In order to decide for yourself, you must understand how a flea collar works.

A flea collar is a plastic strip that is coated with an insecticide. It is worn around the neck of a dog. Over a several-month period, the collar will slowly release the insecticide, which kills fleas. A very low dose will also be absorbed by the dog. A flea, feeding on the animal, will ingest the insecticide.

Tests prove the flea collars do kill fleas. The problem is that they do not repel fleas and will not immediately kill the fleas on the dog. In order to be killed, a flea would need to be exposed to the insecticide for a period of up to three days. You cannot count on a flea to sit on your pet for the required amount of time. It can have a meal at your dog's expense and then hop off to find another place to live. If the flea is not on the dog, the collar will not work.

Flea collars can be effective, though. If your dog is a small, indoor animal and is exposed to very few fleas, a collar may be sufficient to control the problem. On the other hand, if your dog is a large animal or one that is outdoors a great deal of the time, a flea collar will not be able to cope. However, if used with other products, it can help you control your flea problem.

If you decide to use a flea collar, remove it from the package and let it air out for a day. Then, buckle it loosely around your pet's neck, leaving room for three fingers. Check the neck area daily for signs of irritation. A flea collar should not be used on any animal that is young, sick or pregnant.

It is important that any excess be cut off after the collar has been fitted. Since the entire collar has been coated with insecticide, removing the excess will customize the amount of chemicals applied to your pet. If you leave the entire collar on, your dog may be overexposed to the insecticide and become ill.

Sprays and Powders

Sprays and powders are good products. They are more powerful than flea collars, have a longer residual effect than shampoos and are less potent than dips. They are especially effective for short-haired animals. The spray or powder can usually penetrate the coat and get down to the skin. When using a spray or powder on your dog, you can cover most of the animal and can see exactly where you are putting it.

There are some drawbacks, though. Continued use over time can lead to a toxic build-up in the animal. A spray that is alcohol-based will sting open sores on the animal. Powders do not sting but can absorb the oils in the hair, leading to a dried-out coat and skin. Also, both sprays and powders are often accidentally inhaled and can be irritating. And they do not always work on long-haired animals. The insecticide often does not get through the thick coat and ends up sitting on the hair.

The biggest problem can be getting the insecticide onto your pet. It is almost an impossible job to powder or spray a dog that is struggling. You often end up covered with the insecticide while the furious dog darts off, still full of fleas.

The objective is to put the flea product onto the dog's skin without getting it into the eyes or mouth. Spray products are easier. With an adjustable trigger sprayer on top of the container, you can control the volume of each spray as well as the direction. You should set the stream to be one that is relatively localized. You do not want the mist to be so fine that it floats into the eyes. On the other hand, you do not want the stream to be so concentrated that the force of the spray stings the dog.

With a powder, you probably should put the product on your hands and then apply it to the animal. If you try to sprinkle the powder directly on the dog, you often get too much in one place. It then becomes a messy procedure to distribute the insecticide evenly over the dog. Both your pet and you might end up inhaling it.

Whether you are using a spray or powder, there are a few things to keep in mind. First, you should start by applying the insecticide on the dog's head, ears and neck. This puts a barrier around the neck that will keep fleas from running up to the head while you are treating the rest of the dog. When working in this area, you should rub the chemical on by hand or with a cloth, whether using a spray or powder. This method ensures that you do not inadvertently get any into the eyes or mouth.

Second, do not forget to treat the animal's feet and tail. If these areas are not covered, the escaping fleas will run and hide there.

Last, you should always wear gloves. The absorption of toxic chemicals can make you sick. If you choose not to wear gloves, be sure to thoroughly wash your hands after completing the job.

Shampoos and Dips

Shampoos and dips are similar in that a dog is literally bathed in both of the products. But that is where the similarities end. A flea shampoo is the mildest form of treatment; a dip is the strongest.

A shampoo rids your pet of the fleas that are on him but has no residual effect. As soon as the product is rinsed off, new fleas can jump on. That drawback, however, is also the advantage. A flea shampoo is an excellent treatment for puppies and animals that are old or ill. It is extremely safe. And, not only does it rid the dog of his fleas, it also leaves him with a clean coat.

Of all the flea products, dips are the most effective. They are insecticide solutions that are poured over or sponged on a pet and allowed to dry without rinsing. Besides killing fleas, dips help control other external parasites such as ticks, mites and lice.

Dips have a couple of advantages over other forms of flea control. Because you sponge them over the entire animal, you get better coverage of your pet's body than with a spray or powder. This kills more fleas than a powder that will not stay between the dog's toes or a spray that cannot penetrate a thick coat. Because the animal is literally bathed in the dip, you know that the solution has reached his skin. Dips also last longer than other flea products. Flea shampoos have no residual effect; sprays and powders last only three or four days. Dips can often be effective for up to ten days.

However, because dips are so strong, they have disadvantages, as well. You must be extremely careful when using them. The chance of an accidental poisoning is far greater with a dip than with other flea products. When cleaning the coat before applying the dip, you should use a mild shampoo instead of a flea shampoo. In addition, you will have to refrain from using other products, such as a flea collar, for a few days after dipping your dog.

You may not even be able to use a dip. If your dog is a compulsive groomer, he may lick off enough insecticide to become sick. Also, a dog with a heavy flea infestation may have numerous open sores. The wounds may heighten the absorption of the toxic chemicals. You should definitely consult with your veterinarian before dipping your dog.

You should keep one last point in mind. Shampooing or dipping your dog is often an adventurous activity. Since many dogs do not like being wet, you might have your groomer or veterinarian handle this task while you are treating your house and yard.

Other Insecticides

There are two other insecticides that are available only from a veterinarian. They are not applied all over the dog's body. Instead, they are designed to be absorbed by the body and enter the bloodstream. One is a tablet that is given by mouth every third day. The other is a similar insecticide that is applied directly to one small, localized spot on the dog every two weeks; it is absorbed through the skin.

These products are very potent and have different disadvantages and advantages than the traditional insecticide products. First, the products are absorbed into the dog's body and bloodstream. In order for the animal to remain healthy, the insecticide must be broken down by his liver. If the dog has liver trouble, these products cannot be used. Second, they do not repel or kill nonbiting fleas. Instead, they kill only biting fleas. This means that your pet must get bitten for the products to work. So, if your dog is allergic to flea bites, he will still have skin trouble. But since fleas need a blood meal before they lay eggs, no flea that feeds on your pet is able to reproduce. So, the flea population will be reduced over time without the use of other chemicals.

These products are good for cases where humans in the household cannot tolerate exposure to external pesticides or where flea control is especially difficult. But they can only be used on a healthy dog and under veterinary supervision.

Flea Control Without Insecticide

If you have a strong aversion to the use of toxic chemicals or your dog is hypersensitive to insecticides, you might want to try some methods that pose no threat to your pet. Bear in mind that while these are very safe, they are not nearly as effective. They can reduce the current flea population but have no residual effect. Therefore, the frequency of application will need to increase greatly. In most instances, you have to use them every day.

Other typse of flea control products are the repellents such as citrus sprays or citrus shampoos. They are composed of organic materials that are very safe to use. Some have skin conditioners that help control itching. While they do kill a few fleas, they work primarily by repelling them.

A new approach to repelling fleas is to use a collar that emits a high-frequency sound. The sound waves have been shown experimentally to alter the behavior of fleas. You might try one if your pet cannot tolerate a traditional flea collar. However, just like any other flea product, you should watch your dog closely for the first few days after commencing to use an ultrasonic collar. The high-pitched sound may disturb your pet. If you notice any unusual behavior, you should remove the collar and discontinue its use.

A third approach is to add brewer's yeast or garlic to your dog's food. Experiments have not shown these additives to work, even though some people swear by them. Since neither will harm your dog, your veterinarian probably will not object if you want to try them. You should discuss how much to add to each meal with your veterinarian. And even if they do not repel fleas, your pet may still derive some benefit. Many dogs really like the flavor of brewer's yeast and garlic.

One of the most effective noninsecticidal products is the flea comb. A flea comb is a comb with very narrow spaces between the teeth. As you pull the comb through your dog's coat, the fleas will be trapped in the teeth. You can kill the fleas by crushing them or dropping them in a jar of alcohol. In addition to getting the fleas off of your dog, a flea comb has a grooming benefit. It will pull out the dead hair in your dog's coat. You will need to use the flea comb on your dog every day. This may be difficult at first if your dog's coat is very long or thick. But once he gets accustomed to it, he will probably enjoy the daily combing.

Besides protecting your dog, nonchemical means can be used to control fleas in your home. Vacuuming your entire house can be just as effective as using a flea spray or fogger. The problem is that it has to be done on a daily basis. And since the vacuum bag is a good place for fleas to breed, you have to replace the bag after each use. So, while a mechanical means of flea control can be effective, it is not always practical.

Chapter Four
Ticks

If your dog spends much time outside during warm weather, there is a good chance that he will bring home a tick. Ticks are small arachnids related to spiders. The parasites love all warm-blooded animals, but your dog is a prime candidate to have them. A dog does not groom himself as thoroughly as a cat. This trait gives a tick more time to burrow through the coat and embed its head under the skin.

Ticks can be found anywhere there is grass or weeds, bushes or shrubs. They are most common in wooded rural areas, in meadows and on beaches. However, the parasites are known to inhabit city parks, as well. Even your own yard can be a haven for them. As an unsuspecting animal walks by, the ticks can climb on and dig in.

What Ticks Look Like

Ticks come in a variety of shapes and sizes. A tick crawling around on your pet can resemble a fleck of dirt, a sesame seed or even a pebble. Any sudden skin growth that you find on your dog may actually be a tick. When engorged with blood, the parasite may look like a large, fluid-filled cyst.

There is an easy way to differentiate a tick from a growth. If you find a bit of swelling, a cyst, a nodule, a bump or whatever on your pet, you should gently try to turn the lump over. If you can flip it and see legs on the underside, then it is a tick.

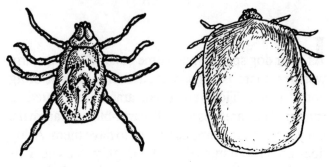

Problems Caused By Ticks

Tick bites can lead to several medical problems. First, the bite of any parasite can cause a skin irritation and possibly result in an infection. Also, if the dog is hypersensitive to ticks, the animal can suffer from a severe allergic reaction. This may generate a general itching fit that will make the dog miserable. In a futile attempt to alleviate the itch, your pet will scratch and bite himself. This can result in hair loss, open sores and infection. A reaction can last for days, even if the tick is removed at once. Hypersensitivity reactions often require veterinary treatment.

Even removing a tick can lead to a skin reaction. Often, a tick that is being pulled out of a host will not release its grasp easily. Even if the proper procedures for tick removal are followed, some of the mouth parts may be left under the host's skin. This will result in an acute, localized inflammation of the bite area. This is usually a minor problem, however. The mouth pieces often work themselves out over the course of a few days. And even if you get the entire tick, it may pull some of the dog's skin with it. A small, open sore will result. This, too, is a minor problem, if the wound is cleaned out properly.

The biggest risk posed by a tick is the transmission of an illness. Ticks can be carriers of several bacterial, viral, protozoan and rickettsial diseases. The most notorious are Lyme disease and Rocky Mountain spotted fever. In addition, tick infestation can lead to anemia, paralysis and other problems with the central nervous system.

Avoiding Tick Bites

The best way to avoid being bitten by a tick is to stay out of the areas where ticks are prevalent. If your particular location has a large tick population, you should probably keep your dog out of heavily wooded areas and any areas with tall grasses. When out walking with him, try to stay on sidewalks or cleared paths. If your dog does not get close to a tick, the parasite will not be able to hop on him.

You should also take steps to keep ticks out of your yard. A clean yard is not as suited to tick infestation as one where the bushes and grass are left to fend for themselves. The grass should be mowed frequently and kept short. Dead branches and shrubs should be cleared. The gardens should not be allowed to become overgrown with weeds.

You can also take steps to protect your dog. A flea and tick collar can help. Since an embedded tick will stay on the dog for a lengthy period, the chemicals in the collar will kill the tick. The only problem is that a flea and tick collar needs several days to complete its task. By that time, the tick may have already transmitted a disease-causing organism. So, other steps should be taken, as well.

One thing that you can do is to put insect repellent on your pet before he goes outside. This might cause some of the ticks that jump on your dog to jump right back off. One problem to avoid, however, is overuse of the insecticide. If your dog goes outside every day, you probably should not douse him with chemicals each morning. That could result in your pet developing a medical problem from over-exposure to the insecticide. Ask your veterinarian to recommend the safest tick repellents.

The most effective way to prevent tick bites is to examine your dog every time that he comes in from outside. A tick check is simple. Ticks have a tendency to bite in areas that are hard for the dog to reach and see. The areas most susceptible are the face, ears, neck, shoulders, legs and toes. Run your hands over the animal's body, feeling for any bumps. A bump with legs is a tick.

It can be tedious to check your pet by hand. A fine-toothed flea comb can help. When a flea comb is run through your dog's coat, it will catch on the larger ticks. The tiny ticks that look like flecks of dirt will often be pulled out along with the hair trapped in the comb's teeth. If your dog hates being combed, try using a sticky-tape lint roller. It will pick up ticks that are crawling on his coat. However, you will still need to look for ticks that may already be embedded.

How To Remove a Tick

A tick may feed on your dog for a period ranging from a few hours to several days. Eventually, after it has finished, it will drop off on its own. However, you should remove any tick found on your pet as soon as possible. Research has shown that it often takes several hours, possibly even a day or so, for an infective tick to transmit enough of a disease-causing organism to result in an illness. The sooner that the parasite is removed, the less chance it has of causing a serious problem.

Removing a tick is not difficult if you know how to do it properly. Some popular methods believed to be effective simply do not work. First, you cannot unscrew a tick from your pet. Ticks do not wind themselves into an animal. If you try this method, you will end up twisting the tick in half, leaving a good portion of it in your dog.

Next, burning a tick with a hot match or a lighted cigarette rarely works. The theory is that the heat will cause the tick to release its grip and back out. What most often happens is that you end up with a scorched but still embedded tick and a dog with a nasty burn.

Also, do not douse a tick with gasoline, kerosene or turpentine. These solutions can be toxic to your dog. If nothing else, they are bad for his skin.

Lastly, some people use petroleum jelly to kill the tick while it is on the dog. Since the parasite exchanges oxygen through its body, it will suffocate if the body is covered. The dying tick is supposed to let go of its hold before it expires. Unfortunately, you usually end up with a suffocated, petroleum jelly-covered tick that is still locked on your pet.

There is a simple and correct way to remove a tick. First, put gloves on. This will reduce the chance of contracting a disease from handling the tick. Next, clean the bite area by dabbing it with alcohol. Use tweezers to grab the tick as close as possible to your dog's skin. Pull slowly and firmly to remove the parasite. With steady pressure, the tick will probably release its grip. Do not yank it out; give the tick time to let go.

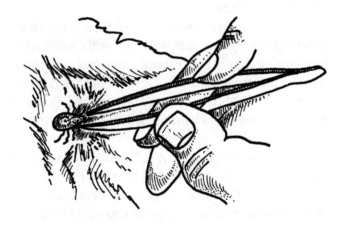

Once it has been removed, do not squeeze the tick's body. This could release any microscopic organisms that are inside the parasite. Instead, kill the tick by placing it in a jar of alcohol. Clean the wound left behind with soap and water. Then, put a mild antibiotic ointment on it. And be sure to wash your hands when finished.

As mentioned earlier, do not be concerned if part

of the tick remains in the skin. Your dog may have a slight skin reaction, but the tick will not regenerate and the mouth parts will not migrate deeper. After the wound is cleaned and disinfected, it will usually clear up in a few days. However, if the area festers and enlarges, you should take the animal to your veterinarian. Most likely, your dog has developed an infection and may require antibiotics.

Should your dog have more than a few ticks, it might be best to use a tick dip to remove them. Start by bathing the animal with a mild shampoo and rinsing him off completely. Then, while the dog is still wet, sponge or pour the dip onto him. A dip is not rinsed off; let the animal drip dry. The dip will kill the embedded ticks and protect your pet for a few more days. Since flea and tick dips are the same product, you should limit the use of any other insecticide during the residual period. Do not put a flea collar back on the dog for the first few days after it has been dipped.

If you live in an area where tick-borne diseases are prevalent, you might want to save the ticks removed from your dog. They can be preserved in small vials of rubbing alcohol. Be sure to record the dates that you found them. Then, if your dog shows any signs of illness, you can have the parasites tested as carriers.

One new development has brought good news in the fight against tick diseases. Dogs in high-risk areas for Lyme disease can be vaccinated against the illness. You should discuss that possibility with your veterinarian.

Chapter Five
Allergies

During the spring, you might notice that your dog is scratching constantly. There is a very good chance that this uncomfortable condition is due to a flea infestation. But it may be something else. Your pet might have an allergy.

An allergy is an overreaction of the immune system to something that the body sees as foreign. Just as for a person, the symptoms exhibited by a dog can vary, depending upon what caused the reaction. And just as for a person, an allergy can make his life miserable.

Signs of an Allergy

While the typical allergic responses for a human are sneezing, coughing and itchy eyes, the primary reaction for a dog is a general itchy condition. The skin has a limited number of ways to respond to irritants. So, regardless of what caused the allergy, most dogs scratch and bite themselves. The most likely areas of concentration are around the face, ears and feet. If your dog has an allergy, he might drag his muzzle along the ground in an attempt to relieve the itch around the ears and eyes.

This can lead to recurrent ear infections. Constant scratching of the ear can result in an inflamed ear canal. Inflammation generates moisture, which in turn, precipitates the growth of bacteria. In a short period of time, the ear is infected. The same holds true for eye infections. They can be triggered by the continuous rubbing of the face and eyes.

Another sign is frequent licking of the feet. Even if you do not see your dog licking his feet, you may suspect it if you notice that the hair around the pads and toes has turned brown. A dog's saliva contains a protein that stains the hair follicles. Excessive licking deposits a large amount of saliva on the feet; this results in discoloration.

Licking can be a problem because the rough surface of your dog's tongue can irritate the skin. This can lead to inflammation and open sores. In addition, the saliva keeps the area between the toes wet, setting the stage for a bacterial infection.

Types of Allergies

For dogs, the most common allergy is to fleas. When a flea bites to feed on a dog's blood, it injects some of its saliva into the dog. For those allergic to the saliva, its injection can set off an intense general itching episode that can last for several days. In a futile attempt to alleviate the condition, a dog may pull out his hair and damage his skin. This, in turn, leaves him highly susceptible to infections.

You may be able to control the number of fleas by using a sound strategy like those discussed in Chapter Three (see page 33). Despite your best efforts, however, a few fleas may get through. And one bite from a single flea can set off an allergic reaction.

Another common affliction is an inhalant allergy. This is a reaction to a substance the dog inhales. The usual culprits are the pollens and spores produced by blooming trees, plants and flowers in the spring. A dog may also be allergic to the flowers' fragrances and growing molds. When you notice that hay fever is in full swing, take a close look at your pet. If he is exhibiting any of the signs mentioned above, there is a good chance that he is having a reaction to something that he inhaled.

The only good thing about this type of allergy is that it is seasonal. Your dog can suffer only when the particles that cause a reaction are aerosolized. When the trees and flowers stop producing the afflicting substance, the symptoms will subside, at least until the next season.

A third type of hypersensitivity is a contact allergy. Certain substances, usually in plants and grasses, cause reactions when an allergic animal comes in contact with them. This results in local inflammation that often consists of redness, bumps, sores and very itchy skin. The contact is made as the dog walks or runs through high grass or underbrush. The underside of the animal is often involved. The area most prone to reaction is the abdomen because it is the part of the dog with the least amount of hair. That makes it more likely that the offending substance will be able to penetrate the coat and make contact with the skin.

An advantage that a canine has over a human is that he does not react adversely to poison ivy. A dog is not usually sensitive to its oils or the oils of poison oak and sumac. However, he can carry the oils on his coat. If you pet your dog after he has romped in a patch of poison ivy, you might end up with a bad skin reaction.

A dog can also have contact allergies that are non-seasonal and not related to outside vegetation. In rare cases, dogs have a reaction to a plastic food bowl. When they are eating, their chins and snouts will continually bump against the bowl. These sensitive dogs will develop a hairless or inflamed area on their chins and faces. If your pet has this condition, you should consider changing to a ceramic or metal bowl.

One product that dogs are commonly allergic to is the flea collar. If your dog is hypersensitive to the insecticide in the collar, you will notice hair loss or a rash on his neck. The affected area can be much wider than the actual collar itself and may extend upwards to the ears and downwards to the back. If you do see a skin reaction, remove the flea collar at once.

The fourth type of allergy is a food allergy. People with a food allergy will develop hives or have diarrhea if they eat something that they should not. It is more difficult to pinpoint an animal's food allergy. A pet may react by developing digestive tract trouble, such as vomiting or diarrhea. He may also exhibit behavioral problems by becoming hyperactive or more aggressive. Or the only evidence may be similar to the symptoms of other allergy problems; he will have chronically dry, flaky, itchy skin.

Testing For Allergies

If you think that your dog may be allergic to his

food, you can perform a test yourself. You can put your dog on an elimination diet. The idea is to eliminate the food that is causing a reaction by changing to another diet made up of items that your dog does not normally eat. If his condition improves after a few weeks, you then put him back on his regular diet. If the symptoms recur, you can assume that he is allergic to something in his usual food. Then, you should consider a permanent change to a commercial hypoallergenic diet that is available from most veterinarians. As long as the new diet is balanced, your dog should do quite well on it.

Before starting your dog on an elimination diet, you should check first with your veterinarian. The doctor may give you advice on how to best handle the switch or have a better way to test for the allergy. Also, you should read the label of your dog's food to identify its ingredients. In the past, you could start an elimination diet by feeding your dog lamb and white rice. However, some dog foods today have lamb and rice components in them. If so, you should ask your veterinarian for a different mix of food for the test.

Your dog can be tested for other types of allergies, too. In many respects, veterinary medicine parallels that for humans. For example, skin testing can determine if your dog has a contact or inhalant allergy. This test will also pinpoint the substances that are causing the reactions.

When you take your dog to the veterinarian for allergy testing, the first step that the doctor takes is to find out if another problem may be the source of the dog's medical troubles. Since a dog's skin has only a limited number of ways to respond to many problems, his constant itching could be the result of a number of things. Your veterinarian first looks for external parasites like fleas, mites or lice. If that proves negative, the doctor may then check for internal parasites that can cause dull coats and scratching. After that, bacterial and other infections will be investigated by performing a skin scraping, culture and possibly a biopsy. That will also rule out tumors and other growths on the skin. If the cause is still not found after taking those steps, your veterinarian may recommend a skin test.

This procedure is similar to allergy testing on humans. The veterinarian clips your dog's side and then injects about thirty to forty different substances, including pollen from different trees and grasses, molds, shrubs, plants and dust. By measuring the dog's reactions to the test injections, the doctor will know exactly what is causing the allergy.

Blood tests are also available to test for allergies. These are quicker, cheaper and easier than skin testing. Unfortunately, they are not yet as accurate as the skin tests.

Allergies Are Controllable

Once the substance that causes the allergy is known, your veterinarian will discuss possible remedies with you. The first step is to keep your dog away from the allergy-causing substance as mush as possible. So, if he is allergic to ragweed growing in a field, walk somewhere else. If he has contact allergies to grass, keep him out of the back yard. If he is allergic to more than one substance, limiting exposure to even one may significantly reduce his reactions.

Your veterinarian may also prescribe a serum to control the allergy. You can easily give the weekly shots to your dog at home or you can take the animal to the clinic for the injections. To be effective, the shots need to be given on a year-round basis, even if the allergy symptoms are evident for limited periods of time.

Another possible solution is very simple. Your veterinarian and you may decide to simply treat the symptoms rather than the allergy itself. This makes sense if the allergies are seasonal. If you can control your dog's discomfort with medication for the two months of the year that he has symptoms, there is no reason to go through the elaborate process of skin testing and weekly serum injections.

Your veterinarian may prescribe antihistamines and corticosteroids. Some of the over-the-counter medicines available in drugstores might also help. However, since the dosages vary and there can be side-effects with these drugs, they should be used only with the consent of your veterinarian.

Chapter Six
Stings & Bites

With the coming of spring, the insect and spider population will soar. You will probably find several species of insects and arachnids in your yard, the parks and other places where you take your dog. A few may even get inside your house. Many dogs like to play with insects and spiders. It may be very funny to watch your pet clumsily chase an agile bee around your yard or a deft spider across the floor. But often, the outcome is not funny. Your dog might get stung or bitten.

Stinging Insects: Bees, Wasps and Hornets

The insects that pose a stinging threat to your dog are bees, wasps, hornets and ants. Most of these insects live in colonies. Curious or playful dogs have a tendency to stir up the members of a community by exploring or falling into the hives or nests. The animal then runs the risk of being stung by several members of the angry group and often several times by an individual insect. Only the honeybee and a few types of wasps, which leave the stinger and venom sac in their victim, can sting just once.

Dogs react to insect stings just like people do. If a dog is lucky, the reaction will be localized. This means that the animal gets a firm, painful, red swelling at the site of the sting. Also, heat is generated by inflammatory products in the blood congregating in the area.

If you are not lucky, your dog will have an allergic response to the insect sting. This can occur immediately after the incident or develop over a period of several minutes to hours. This allergic response is characterized by a great deal of swelling and pain. The swelling can extend far beyond the local area of the sting.

Animals that have been stung previously may suffer from a severe allergic response called an anaphylactic reaction. This is a life-threatening condition caused by the body's immune system. The immune system, having been previously exposed to the insect's toxins, is geared up to combat the venom. The problem is that it overreacts with subsequent exposure. In its effort to overcome one type of emergency, the immune system creates another more dangerous one.

If this happens, there is a tremendous amount of swelling. Your pet's face and throat can swell to the point that the airways contract. Breathing becomes difficult, resulting in the reduced effectiveness of the respiratory and cardiovascular systems. Blood pressure drops and the blood begins to pool. If the body organs do not get an adequate supply of oxygenated blood, the dog will go into shock. When the oxygen supply to the brain drops significantly, the animal will lapse into a coma. In extreme cases, the dog will die.

The best way to prevent a possible allergic reaction is to reduce the chance that your dog will encounter a stinging insect. You should check your yard for bee, hornet and wasp nests. These are often found in woodpiles, under the eaves of houses and behind gutters. These colonies can also be found on the ground. Most hardware stores and grocery stores carry products that will enable you to safely eradicate both the insects and their dwellings. And avoid feeding your dog outdoors because the food attracts insects. If you must, pick up the bowl immediately after he eats.

What To Do If Your Dog Is Stung

If your dog is stung by an insect, you should begin treatment at once. If the assailant was a honey-bee, the first step will be to remove the stinger and venom sac if they are still in the dog. You should do this as quickly as possible. A pulsating venom sac will be pumping more venom into your dog. The amount of venom injected will depend on how long the stinger and sac remain on your pet. Less venom means less swelling and a lower chance for a dangerous reaction.

Try to scrape the stinger out of the skin. You should use a dull-edged object, such as a credit card or the back side of a table knife. If the stinger was inserted at an angle, you should scrape away from the direction that it is pointing. Place the dull-edged object in front of the stinger and venom sack. Then push it across the surface of the skin and the stinger. Hopefully, you will be able to snag the stinger at the point where it joins the venom sac and pull both of them out.

Or, you can use tweezers. If you do, grasp the stinger at the point of entry to the skin. Pull it straight out using steady, even pressure. Do not grasp the stinger by the venom sac and pull out. The stinger will come out, but you will inject more venom into your dog.

Once the stinger is out, treat the swelling with ice packs. Some people recommend putting a paste made of baking soda and water on the site. Even if your dog does not have a severe reaction, you should contact your veterinarian. The doctor may have some advice that will help your dog cope with the discomfort of localized swelling.

On the other hand, if your pet appears to be having trouble breathing or if there is an unusual amount of swelling, you are in an emergency situation. If the swelling extends more than an inch or so from the sting site, you must go to your veterinarian immediately. Do not wait to see how much more the area will swell. Also take your dog to your veterinary clinic if the sting is on the face, mouth, lips, tongue or neck. Your veterinarian will want to put the animal on medication to limit swelling in these areas and prevent potential respiratory problems.

Do not waste time trying to administer a home remedy for the allergic response. While antihistamines made for people can be used for a dog, they are not safe or effective unless given in the proper dose. And the medication may not help your dog much anyway. A medication given orally may take too long to get into the animal's system. By the time that it starts to take effect, your dog could be at the clinic where the same medication could be given via an injection. An antihistamine in injectable form gets into the bloodstream faster; thus, it is more effective. And your veterinarian will know the proper dose to give for your dog's particular condition. Your veterinarian can also administer other medications to limit the allergic response, reduce pain and prevent infection.

Once the emergency is over, your veterinarian and you should discuss precautions to take that may prevent the situation from happening again. The doctor may provide you with injectable medication to keep on hand. As mentioned earlier, a dog that did not suffer an allergic response from one bee sting may experience a severe reaction to the next. And if an animal had a bad generalized reaction once, you must assume that it will happen again. In the event of another sting, you may be able to lessen the danger of a major reaction by administering an antihistamine or other medication at home before transporting the victim to the clinic.

Biting Insects and Spiders

Biting mosquitoes, ants and flies can also bother your dog. Mosquitoes carry heartworm. Both mosquito and ant bites can result in allergic reactions. Dogs allergic to insect bites will have generalized itching that may require veterinary treatment. You can help reduce the number of mosquito bites by eliminating the pools of stagnant water that serve as breeding grounds, keeping your dog inside at dusk (the peak mosquito hours) and investing in an electronic bug killer. Anthills may be eradicated temporarily by pouring boiling water into the nest or by mixing the occupants of one nest into another. Insect repellents approved by veterinarians can be useful.

Biting flies are a nuisance as well. They irritate a dog's eyes and ears, leading to sores and infections. The flies also lay eggs in open wounds; these eggs hatch into maggots. You can limit your pet's exposure to biting flies by keeping debris and garbage cleaned up, putting food bowls away and providing shelter for your pet. Sick and debilitated pets should not be left lying outside as they are easy targets for flies. You can also apply fly repellent to your dog's ears before he goes outside; it is available from your veterinarian.

Spiders can also inflict painful bites on a dog. If your pet is bitten, you might not even know it. The bite marks are usually very small and hidden by the animal's coat. However, if there are many spiders in the area, you should periodically examine your dog closely. You may notice an inflamed, swollen, painful area where a bite occurred.

Besides localized discomfort, the effects of most spider bites do not warrant concern. However, two spiders can be dangerous. One is the black widow. This spider can inject enough venom in its victims to cause abdominal pain and neurotoxic problems such as muscle spasms, convulsions, ataxia and even paralysis. In rare but extreme cases, a dog can die. There is antivenin for the black widow venom, but it must be given very soon after the bite. Usually, an animal bitten by a black widow is treated symptomatically with medications such as corticosteroids and fluids.

The second spider to be wary of is the brown recluse. This spider is prevalent in the southern half of the United States. It is often found in out-of-the-way areas such as a storage bin or the corner of a basement. The concern with the bite of the brown recluse is that the skin around the bite area does not heal. While small initially, the area can expand into a large, painful open wound. Other signs include fever, weakness and vomiting. A dog bitten by this spider would receive supportive treatment. In addition, the animal may need surgery to excise the damaged area and repair the wound.

Preventing spider bites is difficult, especially if you are in an area where arachnids are prevalent. You can try to keep your dog out of the dark recesses of the basement and other out-of-the-way places that arachnids hide. Also, check produce before you bring it into the house; brown recluse spiders may travel into your home in fruit packages and crates. But even with these steps, your dog may still come in contact with spiders. Your best course of action is to examine your pet regularly. If you discover any inflamed, swollen areas, you should contact your veterinarian.

Other Types of Bites and Stings

Depending upon where you live, your dog may be susceptible to other types of bites and stings. Hunting dogs and even house pets can encounter snakes. Most snakes are not poisonous but their bites can still cause problems. Non-poisonous snake bites may result in localized swelling, pain and infection. And no matter where you live, you need to be wary of poisonous snakes; these are found in all parts of the United States. Signs of a venomous snake bite include difficulty breathing and swallowing as well as excess salivating and swelling. If you believe that your dog has been bitten by a venomous snake, you should keep him calm, quiet and warm. He should be taken to your veterinarian as soon as possible. The doctor can administer antivenin and give supportive care. If you have a hunting dog or one that spends a great deal of time outdoors, you should consider getting a snake bite kit. Your veterinarian can recommend the best one for your particular needs.

In desert climates, your pet may come across a scorpion. Like a spider, a scorpion is an arachnid whose sting will leave an inflamed, swollen area that is painful to the touch. The stings of some scorpions are not dangerous. The pain will subside after a short period of time. Others are toxic. They can have general systemic effects such as excessive salivation, vomiting, weakness and even paralysis. Antivenins are available, but they are effective only if given shortly after the dog was stung. If you suspect that your dog has been stung by a scorpion, you should apply a cold compress to the inflamed area and take the animal to your veterinarian for treatment.

If you live near a wooded area, you may have porcupines nearby. Many curious dogs get porcupine quills stuck on their faces and heads. These should be removed as quickly as possible. If not, the quills can begin to migrate further into the body. They cause damage during the migration and can end up embedded in a vital organ.

You should not try to remove the quills yourself. Each quill has thousands of tiny barbs that point backwards. These do not impede the quill from moving deeper, but they do make it very difficult to pull it out. Removing them is a painful process for the dog and dangerous for you. Your pet may violently resist your efforts to help him; you may end up being bitten. Both the animal and you would be better off if your veterinarian removes the quills. It is often necessary to put the dog under a general anesthesia to perform this task. The animal is also put on medication to prevent infection and monitored closely for signs of a missed quill migrating somewhere in the body.

Chapter Seven
Heartworm

As the weather warms up, mosquitoes appear. Their bites are a nuisance to us, but they can be much worse for dogs. Mosquitoes spread a deadly parasite known as heartworm.

What is Heartworm?

For years, veterinarians have been warning us about the dangers of heartworm disease. As the name implies, the heartworm is a worm. However, unlike the worms that typically infect dogs, this parasite does not live in the intestines but in the heart and blood vessels.

In their immature microscopic stage, heartworms are carried by mosquitoes and can be injected into a dog through bites. They mature in the body's connective tissue and then migrate via the bloodstream to the heart, the lungs and the major blood vessels of the respiratory system. They grow to adulthood (six to eight inches long) in about six months. Once mature, they begin to reproduce, creating thousands of tiny offspring called microfilariae. These circulate in the bloodstream throughout the dog. At this point, if a mosquito bites the dog, it may pick up some of the microfilariae and carry them to the next victim.

These heartworms eventually end up back in the heart, lungs and blood vessels, where they will mature and reproduce. As the number of worms grows, they begin to damage the lungs, clog the heart and restrict the flow of blood. This leads to severe heart and lung disease, which can result in heart failure.

Any dog can get heartworm. Do not think that your dog will not be infected because he spends most of the day sleeping on your couch. Every dog goes outside sometimes. All it takes is one mosquito bite from a carrier to infect your dog.

Signs and Treatment

In the early stages, you may not see any signs of heartworm in your pet. Symptoms do not usually appear until the worms are mature, approximately six months after infection. At the time, your dog may start to cough, tire easily, collapse, lose weight, and have trouble breathing.

Treatment is dangerous. An arsenic compound is used to kill the mature worms. After the parasites are dead, the body has to remove them. Unlike intestinal worms which are excreted in feces, dead heartworms settle in the lungs where they eventually decompose. This process can take six to eight weeks. During this period, the dog must be kept quiet. If he becomes stressed or overexerts himself, he may stir up the dead worms, which can damage the heart, lungs or blood vessels. This can cause organ failure and death.

In addition, the arsenic compound used to kill the worms can be harmful. After the worms are dead, the poison must be broken down in the liver. However, if the arsenic causes the liver to malfunction, the dog may not survive the initial stage of treatment.

Treatment is also very expensive. The dog is hospitalized for several days. He undergoes a series of injections and close monitoring using blood tests, x-rays and EKG's. If he recovers, he will receive additional medication to eradicate the microfilariae.

Preventing Heartworm

It is much easier and safer to prevent heartworm than to treat it. This is done by giving your dog preventive medication prescribed by your veterinarian whenever there are mosquitoes in the air. In most areas, the heartworm season begins in the spring and ends in the late fall. In many warm-weather locales, however, the dogs need to be given the medication year-round.

The first step is a blood test. It will determine whether your dog is infected with the parasite. This is crucial. Giving an infected dog preventive medicine is very dangerous. The animal may experience a severe reaction, go into shock and die.

All dogs should be tested at least once a year. For dogs that live in climates that have cold winters, the test should be conducted every spring before the first mosquitoes appear. Dogs that live in warmer regions should have the heartworm test twice each year. Even if your dog is on heartworm medication year-round, he should be tested. No medicine is 100 percent effective. Despite your best efforts, your dog could still contract heartworm disease and need treatment.

A positive test shows the tiny microfilariae in the bloodstream. These immature worms are the offspring of other heartworms. This means that mature worms are in the dog's system. Since worms need six months to mature and the test is performed before mosquito season starts, your pet had to have been infected during the previous mosquito season.

A negative test indicates that your pet is worm-free. You can then take steps to keep him from being infected during the coming season. Depending upon what type of treatment you use, the preventive medicine kills the microscopic heartworms either as they are being injected by mosquitoes into your dog or shortly afterwards. In this manner, heartworms are eradicated before they mature inside the heart and wreak serious damage. The dosage is determined by the weight of your pet.

Types of Heartworm Medication

There are two basic types of heartworm medication. One is given daily and the other is given monthly. The daily medication is very effective and has some residual benefits. Besides preventing heartworm infection, daily pills help control some intestinal parasites, as well. This medication kills the worms as they are being injected, so it must be in the dog before he is bitten by a carrier mosquito.

The problem with daily medication is its required frequency. A dog cannot store the medication in his body. And the medicine will not kill the microfilariae once they are established. So, your dog's protection must be replenished every single day of the mosquito season. Missing just one day can allow the heartworms to infect your pet.

If you use a daily medication, you will need to make administering it part of your everyday routine. You might give it as part of the meals or medicate the dog after his daily walk or before going to bed. The key is to be consistent. Once giving the medication becomes routine, you will be able to remember without even thinking about it. But if you go out of town, you have to make sure that your kennel or pet sitter gives the medication as scheduled.

Another problem with the daily medication is that many dogs resist swallowing pills. The idea of having to go through this ordeal every day can be daunting. To get around this dilemma, other types of medications are now available. One is a flavored, chewable pill. Many dogs love the taste and view the pill as a treat. Daily heartworm medication also comes in liquid form.

More convenient than the daily medication is the type that is given on a monthly basis. If your dog actively resists swallowing pills, it is easier to coax him once every thirty days instead of once every day. This medication is also available in chewable tablets.

There is one important factor to remember when using the monthly medication. It does not kill the heartworms for the next four weeks; it kills the heartworms that were injected by mosquitoes during the previous month. Therefore, you must continue the prevention program for one month after the disappearance of mosquitoes. For instance, if mosquito season ends in November, you need to give your dog heartworm medicine during December. The pill that you gave him in November eradicated the worms injected during October bites. The November worms will be killed by the December medication.

Giving Pills

Prevention sounds very simple until you try to get the preventive medicine into the dog. Some dogs will not allow you to give them any medication, despite your best efforts. It can become a contest of wills that leads to you being frustrated and your pet being angry. A dog that is sufficiently annoyed may may be difficult to handle. So before giving him a pill, position your dog so that he cannot back up. Place a large dog in a sitting position with his back to a wall. A small dog can be put on a table next to a wall.

Open the mouth. Put one hand on the dog's muzzle. The thumb should be just behind one of the two large canine teeth, the index finger behind the other. Tilt the head back. Pull the jaw down with the other hand.

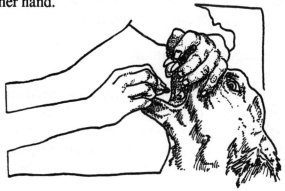

Drop the pill as far back on the tongue as possible. Touch the pill quickly and gently with the tip of your finger. Close the mouth and rub the throat until the dog swallows. You may also try blowing on your dog's face; that often startles the dog and he will swallow by reflex. Open the mouth to see if the pill went down. If it did not, repeat the process.

If you are having difficulty giving heartworm or any other medicine, you might try an alternative method. The best plan is to get five or six morsels of food, such as cheese or peanut butter. Hide the medication in one of them. Then give your dog one or two pieces that do not have have the pill in them. Your pet will probably chew the first few morsels to find out exactly what they are. Once he realizes that they are treats that he loves, he will swallow the remaining morsels without chewing. However, be sure to check that the dog did swallow the pill with the treat. Some animals are very adroit at separating the two.

Another possibility is to grind the pill and mix it in with the dog's food. You must make sure, however, that your pet eats all of his food at once. If he leaves a portion in the feed bowl, he will not be getting the proper dose of medication.

Giving Liquid Medication

The easiest method of giving liquid heartworm medication is to mix it in with the dog's meal. This works as long as the dog eats the entire portion of food. You can also give liquid medication by hand.

Open the dog's mouth using the same technique

shown for giving pills. The only difference is that the head should be kept level. It should not be tilted back as for giving a pill. Squirt a small amount of the liquid into the side of the mouth. Do not squirt it into the back or the medication may go down the windpipe instead of the throat. Close the mouth and rub your dog's throat until he swallows. After he has swallowed, repeat the process until you have given the complete dosage.

If you have trouble getting your dog's mouth open, you can try pulling the lips away from the gums. Then you can squirt the medication a little at a time into the small space created there.

Chapter Eight
Reproduction

Spring is the season of birth and renewal. It is the time when new life bursts from all living beings. While the creation of new life is a beautiful and wondrous process, it is not always welcome. This is especially true for pets.

The Need For Population Control

There are just not enough good homes for all of the puppies born. A female canine begins the reproductive cycle at about six months of age. At that time, she can become pregnant, resulting in a litter that usually numbers between one and twelve puppies. If that one female averages only one litter a year, she and her offspring could be responsible for the birth of over 4000 puppies in a seven year time span.

Sadly, most puppies go unwanted and homeless. They either end their lives on the streets or wind up in animal shelters. Over 12 million unwanted pets are euthanized in animal shelters each year. Millions more die from starvation, exposure and injuries sustained when hit by cars. While animal shelters do what they can to place their charges in homes, most of the puppies there will be destroyed after only a couple of weeks.

Just as sad as the fact that these deaths occur is that they do not need to happen. If every dog owner took responsible steps for population control, the birth of many of these adorable but doomed animals could be prevented. And population control is not just the responsibility of the owners of female dogs. The owners of male dogs cannot turn their backs on the situation. Overpopulation is everybody's problem.

Neutering

If you do not plan to breed your dog, you should take steps to ensure that your female does not become pregnant or that your male does not sire a litter. The only way to guarantee that your dog will not contribute to the exploding canine population is to have your pet neutered.

Neutering is the removal of the reproductive organs. For a female, the procedure is known as spaying; it constitutes taking out the uterus and ovaries. For a male, it is called altering or castration; it is the removal of the testicles. For both sexes, it is a surgical procedure that requires that the animal be put under anesthesia.

Neutering usually takes place when the animal is between the ages of six months and one year. Females should be spayed before the first heat cycle. This is when they are approximately six months old.

Males are usually neutered at the far end of the age range. This allows for the continued circulation of the male hormone, testosterone, during the dog's prime growth stage. This aids in the development of male characteristics such as heavy, dense muscling and a large body structure. However, if your male dog is demonstrating dominance, aggression or other undesirable behaviors associated with hormone production, you may want to have him neutered earlier. You should discuss this situation with your veterinarian.

Besides eliminating any chance of an unwanted pregnancy, the procedure has several medical benefits. If your female is spayed before her first heat, she will not have circulating female hormones, estrogen; this results in her being 100 percent protected against the development of malignant mammary cancer later in life. If the procedure is performed after her first heat, the amount of protection is diminished. After the second heat, she will derive no benefit against breast cancer. However, being spayed at any age will eliminate the risk of pyometra, a very serious disease that involves the production of pus in the uterus. In addition, it eliminates the female having the bleeding episodes associated with being in heat. It will also stop male dogs from congregating around the house when your female is in heat. This prevents the spread of contagious diseases and limits the possibility of dog fights and injuries.

Neutered males also derive a medical benefit. Diseases of the prostate in aging male dogs have been related to the presence of testosterone. When a male dog is altered, the chance of developing prostate trouble is reduced drastically.

Both neutered males and females generally have fuller, healthier coats. Removal of the reproductive organs stops the hormonal fluctuations that can result in poor hair condition and hair loss. Once dogs are altered or spayed, they usually resume normal patterns of hair growth.

The only risk associated with neutering is that of medical complications occurring while the animal is under anesthesia. However, the strong heart, lungs and other organs of a young animal make the dog an excellent candidate for surgery. Dogs usually go through the operation with no problems. And the medical benefits far outweigh the risk.

The Fallacies of Neutering

There are several misconceptions about the effects of neutering. It used to be said that a female should go through one heat or she will never fully mature. However, this is not true. Another falsehood is that a female dog must have a litter of puppies to be psychologically fulfilled. Dogs function as pets for people. They are just as oriented toward their human families as they would be towards their offspring. Being spayed actually results in their being more attentive to their human families. Furthermore, spayed dogs do not exhibit any of the behavioral effects caused by hormonal changes associated with the reproductive cycle. Some dogs act ill or uncomfortable while in heat. Spaying also prevents your dog from experiencing a false pregnancy; this is a condition where the dog acts as if she is pregnant. Her nipples will develop and she will act out motherly traits such as nesting and possessiveness. She may also become more aggressive.

Another misconception is that neutering a male

will break his spirit. Altering can have a slight effect on his behavior, but it will not change his basic personality. After having the procedure, a male may tend to be less aggressive and less likely to wander off. However, if your male is altered after he is a few years old, the operation may have no effect on his behavior. By that time, his normal behaviors will have become habits as opposed to instincts governed by hormones. Once they are habits, neutering will not reverse them.

In addition, many people mistake poor handling and inadequate training for hormonal problems. A dog that is extremely active and aggressive towards people before being castrated will probably still be so afterwards. If you cannot control your dog when he is intact, you will not be able to control him when he is altered.

Finally, many people believe that all neutered animals gain weight. Again, this is not the case. Animals put on pounds for the same reasons that people do: too much food, too little exercise. As dogs mature, they need less calories per ppund of body weight than they did as puppies, whether they are neutered or not. If their diets are not reduced to match their level of activity, they will gain weight.

You should discuss neutering with your veterinarian. Once you have all the information, you will realize that a neutered dog is a better pet. And by opting for this procedure, you will have made a responsible decision regarding population control. Remember, you are not hurting your pet; you are preventing many tragic deaths.

Part II

Summer

Chapter Nine
Summer Basics

Summer is a great time of year. The days are longer and everybody seems to take life a little easier. However, the weather that makes humans slow down and relax does create some special needs for your dog. A few simple steps and some common sense can keep your dog healthy and comfortable all summer long.

Water

Far and away, the most important step that you should take during the summer is to ensure that your dog has plenty of fresh water. Water is an essential nutrient; it is needed in every part of the body. It helps the body systems function properly. An adequate water supply maintains the correct blood volume and body pH as well as the proper balance of electrolytes. A dog can live for quite awhile without food, but he cannot survive without water.

As the temperature rises, a dog's body has to work harder, resulting in a more rapid loss of body water. In as little time as one day, he can dehydrate to the point of becoming sick. If he loses more than 10 percent of his body water, he may die.

Your dog, whether he is inside or outside, should have "free choice" access to cool, clean water. He should be able to drink as much as he wants, whenever he wants. If possible, you should replenish his supply several times a day. At the very least, the water in his bowl should be changed every day.

There are a few other things that you can do to help maintain your pet's water supply. First, place the bowl in a shaded area. Water bowls inside your house should not be near windows exposed to direct sunlight. Outside bowls should be put under a tree or overhang, protected from the sun's rays.

Second, use a bowl that is not a good conductor of heat. Stainless steel bowls and many plastic bowls can become very hot if exposed to high heat. The water will warm up and evaporate quicker. A bowl made of clay or ceramics is a better insulator. It will keep the water cooler longer. Putting ice cubes in the water will also help keep the water cold for a short period of time.

Last, the bowl should be secured so that it cannot be moved. When drinking, many dogs push their bowls in all sorts of directions. In their haste, dogs have been known to knock bowls over, spilling their only supply of water. Small, weighty objects can be placed around the bowl to hold it in position. They will also help keep your dog from tipping the bowl over. Depending upon the design of bowl, you may be able to tie it to a fixed object such as a fence post or table leg. You can also buy bowls with non-tip stands and weighted bowls that cannot be tipped over.

Besides plenty of water for drinking, you may want to provide some for cooling the dog's body off. A plastic wading pool is an excellent tool for hot summer days. By lounging in the pool, your dog can keep his body temperature down. And when he gets out, the water evaporating from his coat will have a cooling effect as well.

If you have a concrete dog run, you might hose it down every so often. Concrete holds heat and releases it very slowly. Frequent dousings keep the temperature down and make your dog more comfortable.

Shelter

Besides water, your dog needs shelter. If overexposed to direct sunlight, he may overheat, even if he is inactive. One solution is to keep the dog inside your house. If you are keeping yourself cool, your dog will also benefit from your efforts. However, that may not be feasible when you are not home; you may not want your pet to have free run of the house.

For those times, you may be able to keep your dog inside the house but confined to a room. If your house has central air conditioning, this will certainly be cooler than staying outside. However, if your house is not air conditioned, a closed-up room can heat up rapidly, especially if it has several windows exposed to direct sunlight.

To make the surroundings more comfortable for your dog, lower the shades to block the sun. You should also make sure that the room has adequate ventilation. A fan or two can circulate the air. This will make it seem fresher and aid in cooling.

If your dog cannot stay unsupervised in your house, he can be left outside as long as he has access to shade as well as water. Do not make the mistake of tying the dog in one place and expecting whatever shade he is under to last all day. As the sun moves, the shadows and shade also move. So, the shade tree of the morning may be ineffective against the afternoon sun. Your dog's shelter should be an object, such as a roof or overhang, that blocks the burning rays all day. A tree or a bush may be sufficient as long as your pet can move with the shade and sun. Metal objects, such as a drum or sheet metal overhangs, should be avoided; they overheat rapidly.

The best shelter may be a doghouse. It will keep a dog cooler in the summer and warmer in the winter. What constitutes a good doghouse is discussed in the chapter called "Winter Basics" (see page 196).

There is one issue that may force you to compromise on your selection of a doghouse. When it is cold, the ideal size is one where your dog has just enough room to turn around and lie down. The house is then warmed by his body heat radiating back off of the ceiling and walls. In the summer, however, your dog is better off with more space. This will allow the interior to be cooler and increases ventilation. So, a house that is perfect for summer may be too large for your dog to heat in the winter.

If you do not want to buy a doghouse for summer and one for winter, you will have to make a decision on which size is best for your dog. When making that choice, take into account the severity of the summers and winters in your area. If one season is more extreme than the other, provide your dog with a house more suited for that one. On the other hand, if the two seasons are equally extreme, you should get a house better suited for winter. It is easier to find adequate shelter in the summer than winter. Since your dog will want more space when it is hot, he may be just as happy under a shade tree or an overhang as he would be in a doghouse. When it is cold, he will want a confined area; this is not always readily available.

It is also a good idea to place the house under another shelter. Putting the doghouse in the shade of a tree or overhang will keep the roof and sides cooler. And that will make the interior more comfortable.

Summer Exercise

You may have started your dog on an exercise program during the spring. You should continue it during the summer, but you will have to make some adjustments for the warmer temperatures. First, if you take your dog on daily walks or jogs, you may need to change the schedule. The afternoons are usually hotter than the mornings and evenings. If you walk your dog when you get home from work, you should consider changing your routine to walking him before your leave for work or after dinner. Either one of these times will be cooler.

Second, you probably will have to increase the number of rest and water breaks. Your dog heats up faster than you. If you stop only when you are thirsty or tired, your dog will suffer. In addition, a dog is not necessarily self-regulating; he will push himself to keep up with you, even if he is starting to overheat. It is a good idea to rest and cool down every twenty minutes, whether the dog looks tired or not. He should never exercise for longer than thirty minutes without a break. A dog can decompensate suddenly and suffer heatstroke. With each break, your dog should have plenty of water to drink. If it is not available where you exercise, you should bring water with you.

Third, whenever possible, walk on a grassy surface rather than streets and sidewalks. Hot concrete can burn the pads of your dog's feet. Melting tar can burn the feet, as well. It can also stick to the pads and congeal on the wounds, increasing the risk of infection. On the other hand, the ground absorbs less heat and cools off faster than concrete. In addition, grass is softer and will reduce the amount of stress placed on the joints.

Last, there may be times when you should cancel an exercise and play period with your dog. If it is too hot for you, it will definitely be too hot for your dog, especially if he is overweight or a flat-faced animal. While you will only be very uncomfortable in extremely hot weather, your dog will be extremely hot and overheat. The consequences can be severe. Both of you might be better off taking it easy until the weather cools down a bit.

Swimming

One of the best summer exercises is swimming. Water buoys the body. This reduces stress on the muscles, tendons, joints and ligaments. Also, as the water surrounds the body, it cools and prevents it from overheating. Thus, swimming provides cardio-vascular and aerobic benefits without the risks associated with other summer exercises.

However, animals are just like people; not all of them like the water. You cannot make any assumptions when it comes to water and your dog. Some "water dogs" hate to swim while some "lap dogs" love it. A dog needs to be introduced to water gradually. When exposing your pet to water for the first time, let him explore the water's edge on his own. This way, his curiosity will overcome his fear.

You should not throw your puppy into the drink and expect him to swim. Even though dog paddling is ingrained, most dogs still need to learn how to do it. A dog in the water for the first time does not know that he can swim. He may flail about in an attempt to get out. Some dogs overcome their fear quickly and realize that they can swim. Others, however, may pull with their front legs but not use their hind legs. This causes the dog to stand straight up in the water; he can easily sink. He may be so frightened that he panics. Many panic-stricken dogs drown.

Many dogs learn to swim by watching other dogs. Or, you can teach your dog. The lesson should take place in calm, shallow water. After he is comfortable standing in the water, take him out a few feet from where he can stand comfortably and head him back to the water's edge. If he has a problem, you can buoy him. Once he learns to keep his back end up in the water, he will quickly become an expert swimmer.

You should not engage him in games of fetch

immediately after he learns to swim. It may confuse or disorient him. Wait until he is an expert swimmer before asking him to retrieve objects from the water. In addition, your dog should not go out into the ocean or a river with a current until he has confidence in his newfound skill.

Your dog can swim every day of the summer if you have a pool. However, you will need to take some precautions. Many dogs have jumped into the pool only to discover that they could not get out. Even a strong swimmer will eventually weaken and drown if he cannot find the exit. You must be certain that your dog knows where the stairs are. You should show him several times. If you do it only once, he may forget in his panic to get out. In addition, you should also take steps to keep your dog out of the water unless you are there to supervise. Erecting a small fence around the area will limit his access. If you use a pool cover, it should be strong enough to hold the dog's weight.

While swimming is great exercise, there are a few cautions to follow. First, you should rinse off your dog with fresh water after swimming. The ocean has salt and other minerals. Pools have strong chemicals. Streams and lakes have bacteria such as leptospirosis and giardia. The salt and chemicals can dry the skin; the bacteria may cause illness.

Most importantly, do not let your dog into any water that you would not go in. Just because he has four legs does not mean that he is any better equipped to withstand rapids or undercurrents than you are. If you should not go in, neither should he.

Summer Haircuts

Another summer issue is haircuts. Many dog owners think that they are doing their pets a favor by having their coats shorn for the summer. The rationale is that, without a full coat of hair, an animal will be more comfortable. That assumption, however, is not always correct.

A long-haired dog is actually cooler and safer with his hair at its normal length. It insulates the animal against heat and sun. During the warm months, the coat is usually thinner; the hairs are coarser and wider-spaced. If the hair remains tangle-free, air is able to circulate around the skin. Removing the hair does not make him any cooler, and it increases the dog's exposure to the sun's rays.

On the other hand, dogs with matted hair suffer more in the heat. The tangles provide excellent hiding places for fleas. They also trap dirt, twigs and other debris. This condition can lead to skin infections. If your dog's hair is full of tangles, it should be cut. Otherwise, he is better off with his locks.

If you really want to help him stay cool, give him an extra brushing. That ensures that the hair remains free of mats and conducive to good air circulation.

Chapter Ten
Summer Dangers

Summer means hot weather. While most dogs enjoy sitting in the sunshine, they do not like the heat. They are more prone to complications from overexposure to hot weather than people are. The reason is that dogs heat up faster and take longer to cool down. This can be a deadly combination. You should take steps to prevent your dog from overheating and keep him safe throughout the summer.

Why Hot Weather Is Dangerous

Dogs are not well-equipped to handle hot weather. While their coats insulate them from sun's rays, the hair does act like a sweater by keeping some heat next to their body. Wearing a sweater in July and August certainly contributes to the negative effect of high temperatures.

In addition, dogs have a more difficult time cooling off than people do. They do not have sweat glands; they cannot perspire. Instead, they pant. When hot, a dog breathes in cool air and exhales hot air. Water evaporating off of the tongue also helps the dog regulate his body temperature.

Unfortunately, neither of these methods is always efficient. Your dog's ability to cool himself down diminishes rapidly as the outside temperature goes up. If it gets as high as the animal's internal temperature, there cannot be any heat exchange. Also, high humidity means that less moisture can evaporate off the tongue and from the oral cavity. This, too, hinders the cooling process.

As the temperature and humidity increase, your dog will attempt to cool off by panting harder. The panting causes electrolyte abnormalities within the animal's body, keeping the organs from functioning properly. The dog also suffers from dehydration; this is a decreased amount of body water. Less water will create a change in the blood's viscosity. This impedes proper circulation and makes it harder to maintain the proper level of oxygen throughout the dog's system.

Puppies, older dogs and those that are sick are less able to compensate for these changes. Obese animals are also at risk. And all pets with inadequate water supplies and ventilation are prone to overheating.

Canines with short noses and flat faces have additional problems. Over the years, they have been bred to have short faces. This has altered their upper respiratory apparatus. Simply put, they have the same equipment as other dogs but less space to hold it. As a result, they often have redundant tissue in the throat. Their larynx may not open correctly; they may have skin flaps that close down the nose; their soft palate may hang over the opening to the trachea. Each of these makes breathing more difficult. Such obstacles in an already inefficient cooling system increase the dangers of hot weather.

Heatstroke

The greatest danger faced by a dog in the summer is heatstroke. When a dog is dangerously hot, the blood supply is shunted towards the extremities, where heat exchange is most efficient. In the process, the supply to the organs is depleted. If too much blood is drawn away from organs such as the kidneys, heart and brain, heatstroke will ensue. The animal might collapse and could possibly slip into a coma.

The signs of impending heatstroke are those of a dog overheating. Initially, he will pant excessively and have a rapid heart rate. His nose, legs and ears will be hot. The mouth and tongue can be bright red or purple. As heatstroke develops, the tongue will swell and the animal may develop diarrhea. He will become weak and wobbly. The condition can progress to coma and death.

Heatstroke happens rapidly; it is a dire emergency. The dog must be cooled off at once to avoid permanent damage or death. Move him immediately to a cool, shaded place. If the animal is conscious, offer him tiny amounts of cool water to drink. Do not force it down his throat, especially if he is unconscious. In addition, cover the dog with cool water. You can either run water from a hose over him or put him in a tub. (If you use a tub, be sure to hold the dog's head above the water; if not, it could sink beneath the water and he will drown.)

You should also place ice packs around the body and on his head. It is important, however, that you do not immerse the dog in ice or place ice directly on him. His body cannot compensate for a sudden, severe change in temperature. Also, it may cause a malfunction of the homeostatic mechanism in the brain that regulates body temperature. This will prevent the dog from knowing whether to heat himself up or cool himself down. So, wrap the ice packs in a towel before using them.

You will not be able to adequately treat a heatstroke on your own. After starting the initial cooldown phase, take the animal to your veterinarian as soon as possible. Rapid treatment is critical for recovery. On the way, you should keep ice packs on the animal. You should also gently massage the dog; this will improve the circulation to all areas of the dog's body.

Obviously, it is better to prevent heatstroke than to treat it. One of the easiest ways is to never leave your dog in a parked car. It is the number one cause of heatstroke. The reason that it is so common is that the temperature does not have to be extremely hot in order for a car to become an oven. The interior of a parked car can rapidly heat up as much as 40 degrees above the outside temperature. On an 80-degree day, the inside of your car can reach 120 degrees within minutes. This can happen even with the windows cracked open. No animal can survive in that kind of heat.

Dogs can get heatstroke in other places besides parked cars. Poorly ventilated crates are a frequent site. Pets that are left outside without adequate shelter and water can overheat on a hot day. So can a dog that overexerts himself. This is especially true of animals that jog with their owners and play boisterously with children.

You should take steps to minimize the chance of heatstroke. Whenever your dog is outside, you should limit his activities in the hottest parts of the day. You must also ensure that he has a cool, shaded place to rest. Whenever he is inside your house, he should be in an area with good ventilation. This is especially true if he is confined in a crate. And all dogs, whether inside or out, need to have plenty of fresh water.

Falls

A common accident that occurs in warmer weather is falling. When the weather is nice, many people leave windows open and doors to balconies ajar. When the windows are open, a dog can hear and see more. In his excitement, he may lose some of his normal caution. Since he does not understand the concept of heights, your dog might jump. Or he might fall. A dog that is used to putting his feet up on a window might do this only to discover that the space is open or covered by a flimsy screen.

A dog that jumps or falls out of a window or off a balcony usually goes head first. His front legs hit the ground, often breaking. In addition, a falling dog will often land on his face. This can lead to a concussion and a broken chin and jaw. There can also be serious internal trauma. The lungs can be bruised by the impact. Nerves can be avulsed (torn off) of the spinal cord, leading to paralysis.

Fortunately, reducing the chance of a fall is

relatively simple. If you have a balcony with wide spaces between the railings, you should put up some sort of latticework or wire fence. This will prevent your dog from slipping through. In addition, any window that is left open should have a sturdy screen that is secured tightly. A little nail or hook is not sufficient. In his effort to catch a squirrel in a nearby tree, a frantic dog may pop open a screen. Heavy screws or several hook-and-eye latches can help keep the dog inside, where he belongs.

Sunburns

Believe it or not, some dogs get sunburns. For the majority of canines, their skin is not adversely affected by the sun. It is protected both by their hair and the dark pigment of their skin. The sun might bleach the hair a shade or two lighter. But that sort of change is simply cosmetic and not dangerous.

However, there are a few dogs that are at risk. They are the ones that have pink skin and white hair coats. As a general rule, areas where pink skin can be seen beneath the coat can be burned. If your eyes can reach them, so can the sun's ultraviolet rays.

The most common spots are the extremities; they tend to have less hair coverage than the rest of the body. The nose seems to be at the greatest risk; the ear flaps are frequent burn sites, as well.

Just like sunburn on people, a dog's sunburnt skin will be red and sore. The area can swell and the skin can crust. There can also be hair loss. Chronic exposure to the sun can lead to irritation, blisters, ulcers and infection. Once a pet demonstrates sensitivity to the sun, the conditions usually gets worse over the years, not better. Repeated cases of severe sunburn may develop into skin cancer; this frequently requires amputation of the affected area.

If your dog gets a sunburn, you should treat the animal in the same manner as you would a person. Put ice or cold compresses on the site. Over the course of a few days, the skin should heal. A serious sunburn should be treated by your veterinarian. The doctor can put your pet on antibiotics to prevent bacterial infections and give the animal medication to reduce inflammation and speed healing.

If your dog is susceptible to sunburns, you can help protect him. Limit his exposure to the sun. During the hours when the sun's rays are the strongest, he should be kept indoors.

If you know your dog will be exposed, you can reduce the sun's effect by applying sunscreen to the ears and nose about thirty minutes before going outside. For most dogs prone to sunburns, the entire bridge of the nose should be covered, not just the tip. If you do not have any sunscreen, you can temporarily substitute black shoe polish or a black marker to protect the tip of the nose. Regardless of what you use, you should repeat the application frequently. Most animals tend to lick off foreign substances from their nose. Since ingesting the lotion may make your dog sick, you should keep an eye on him for a while after each application.

There is a permanent solution available for a dog that suffers chronic nose sunburns. A veterinarian can apply dark pigment by tattooing the entire nose with black ink. This may seem like an extreme measure, but it is better than running the risk of skin cancer.

Ear Infections

If your dog swims frequently, there is a good chance that he will get an ear infection. This can interfere with your dog's hearing. A severe case can damage the eardrum, spread into the middle ear and affect your dog's sense of balance. Regardless of the severity, all ear infections have one thing in common; they are painful.

Most swimmer's ear infections are caused by the pooling of water. When it gets inside the ear, water goes down a vertical canal along the side of the face and makes a 90-degree turn towards the inside of the head. Once down there, it does not evaporate easily. Some water dissipates but the lining of the ear stays moist. This moisture can cause the organisms that live inside a healthy ear to overgrow. This overgrowth can cause a clinical infection. In addition, the water may have bacteria or fungi that contribute to the infection.

You should suspect that your dog has an ear infection if you notice a few of the classic symptoms. One early sign is the animal cocking his head sideways. By tilting his head, he is trying to relieve the excess pressure. As the infection worsens, your dog may start shaking his head or pawing at his ears or neck. He might drag the head and ear along the floor.

In addition, the ear and the ear flap will be red and swollen. You may detect a peculiar odor and some fluid discharge. A final sign is the dog's reaction when you touch the ears. If he shies away or cries out, you can bet that an infection has set in.

The sooner that an infection is detected, the easier it will be to treat. You should take your pet to your veterinarian. The doctor will check to see that the eardrum is intact as well as clean and flush out the ear. If the infection is severe, your dog may need antibiotics.

Your veterinarian will probably give you some topical medication that you can use to treat the ear at home. Put medication into the ear canal and then massage below the ear. This will enable the medication to make its way down the canal and across to the eardrum. Afterwards, wipe out any discharge or excess medication with a tissue or cotton swab.

When cleaning the ear, you need to exercise caution. You do not want to go past the vertical part of the ear canal. If you do, you may pack the debris down into the canal and put additional pressure on the eardrum. That could cause it to burst.

You should continue the treatment for as long as instructed by your veterinarian. It may be for a period of several weeks. Ears often respond rapidly to treatment and can appear to be in good shape after only a couple of days. But if you stop too soon, the infection can come back.

The chance of an ear infection can be reduced by cleaning out your dog's ears periodically. This is usually done at weekly intervals but your veterinarian can advise you how often your pet's ears need cleaning. You can use mineral oil or olive oil to dissolve any excess wax build-up in a healthy ear. Or your veterinarian may supply you with medicated cleansers. In addition, you can purchase a drying agent that can be put into the ears after your dog has been in the water. This helps dry the ear canal and kills any bacteria picked up while swimming.

Chapter Eleven
Hot-Weather Travel

Most family vacations take place during the summer. Since your dog is part of the family, you might want to take him with you. Even if your pet stays home each summer, he will travel with you at some time in his life, even if it is only a trip to the veterinarian. Whether it is a trip cross-country or across town, you always take precautions to make your trip safe for you. You should do the same for your dog.

Riding In the Car

Most dogs love to ride in cars. Being with you on an outing and seeing new, exciting sights is a thrill that is hard to beat. However, some dogs do get carsick. They are usually puppies, and they often grow out of the problem. Part of the problem is that the dog is nervous. If your dog has never gone for a ride, he should be acclimated to the concept before embarking on a trip. And if your pet is the nervous type, you can help him get over his fear.

The first step is to introduce your dog to the car before he rides in it. For several consecutive days, put the dog in the car, but leave it parked. He should have a chance to explore the vehicle without being concerned about maintaining his balance. Next, after he is comfortable, you can drive the car around the block. Slowly increase the amount of time the trips take. The objective is to get the dog in and out of the car before he gets sick. He should adjust to the motion after a short period. Then you may have difficulty keeping him out of the vehicle. If he does not adjust, ask your veterinarian to prescribe medication to reduce motion sickness.

Whenever taking your pet for a ride, you have three goals. One is to keep the animal inside the car. If your dog is like most, he will want to hang his head, front paws and even his upper torso out the window. Unfortunately, the dog may fall out. A fall from a moving car can result in serious traumatic injuries and even death. If a dog survives the fall, he might be run over by another vehicle or run away and get lost. Even a dog that stays inside the car is frequently hit by all sorts of flying objects. The result can be eye infections, ear diseases and head trauma. Just leaving his face in the wind is a bad idea; the airflow dries out his mucous membranes and makes his eyes more susceptible to conjunctivitis.

The next objective is to keep the animal under control. A dog that is able to move freely around a vehicle can put everyone in danger. The dog may want to be petted or to play by nipping at your hands and feet. He might lunge at a squirrel or cat outside the car. Or he may examine objects that should be off-limits, such as bags of groceries. Any of these would force you to divert your attention from your driving to regain control of the dog. You must keep your mind and hands free to concentrate on the road.

The third objective is to keep the dog himself

from becoming a flying object in the event of a traffic accident. If the car comes to an abrupt halt, an unsecured dog could go through the windshield. He could also hit another passenger or you. Unless the animal is held by a restraining device, his risk of serious injury or death increases dramatically.

The safest method for transporting a dog is to use a well-ventilated carrier. These are usually constructed of wire mesh. The carrier should be big enough to allow your dog to lie down comfortably, yet small enough to fit conveniently in your car. The airy carrier will still allow your dog the thrill of the breeze blowing by his face and will not obstruct his view. Most carriers can fit easily into the back of a van or station wagon. Many can go on the back seat of a car. If so, you might want to use a seatbelt to secure it. That would be safer in the event of a sudden stop.

If your pet resists going into a carrier, you can use a different method to restrain him. A dog seatbelt might work. This is actually a harness that attaches to a seatbelt. The harness fits around the the dog's chest and back. One end of an adjustable leash fits on the harness; the other end attaches to a seatbelt. The lead should allow the dog a bit of maneuverability. He should be able to lie or sit as he chooses. But he should not have enough slack to extend his head out of a window or get into mischief. Just like a carrier, a harness will keep the dog from becoming a flying object in a wreck.

One type of restraint that should not be used is a collar and leash. While these devices will restrict an animal's movement inside a car, they pose a new danger. If your dog should fall from the car, the force applied to his collar could strangle him. Any restraining device attached to the dog should encircle his chest, not his neck.

If you have a van or station wagon, you might purchase a partition for the back area. It will allow the dog complete freedom of movement but will isolate him from the rest of the vehicle. It will also keep him from jumping out when a door is open. This sort of device is good for confining large dogs.

Another potentially useful item for a small dog is a special car seat. It functions like a car seat for a child. The dog is attached to the seat by a harness and clip; the seat is attached to the car. Since it gives your pet a perch to sit on, he will be able to take in the sights and still be restrained safely.

You should also make sure that your dog is safe when he is left in a parked car. First, you should never leave your dog in a parked car on a warm day. As discussed in the chapter entitled "Summer Dangers," a parked car can heat up dangerously in a very short period of time. Your dog could suffer heatstroke.

However, if the weather does allow you to leave your dog in the car, you must make sure that he has fresh air but cannot get out. This can be accomplished with a window gate. It fits snugly between the top edge of the open window and the door frame. Another benefit is that it prevents people from sticking their hands inside your parked car to pet the animal. This could keep your dog and you from becoming entangled in a complicated biting incident.

If you have a truck, you should not let your dog ride around in the open bed. He may have a great time, but he will not be safe. It is all too easy for a dog to lose his balance whenever the truck turns or stops. Puppies and older dogs often have a difficult time keeping their equilibrium under control. Even an adult dog that has logged hours in a truckbed can stumble if the vehicle makes an unexpected maneuver. In addition, a dog in the back of your truck is more likely to be injured if another vehicle strikes yours.

If you do allow your dog to ride in a truck bed, the animal should be restrained. A secured crate would give your pet a special place to ride. Or, you can use a dog harness. The strip of nylon that connects the harness to the truck should be kept very short. If your dog has enough slack to move the length of the bed, he has enough to go over the side. If that happens, he may be injured by the fall and then dragged along the ground until you can stop. And never secure your dog with a collar and leash. If he falls out, he might be strangled. The animal would be much safer in the truck cab; he should ride up there with you.

Long Trips By Car

Travelling by car with your pet is like travelling with young children. It is never simple; you always seem to need more things than you have room for. But it can be enjoyable, especially if you are going on vacation. Your pet will have a chance to meet new people and see the world from a dog's perspective.

At the very least, a dog that is travelling is

somewhat unsettled. He is away from his home territory and encountering many unfamiliar sights and sounds. To help your dog, you should try to maintain as much of his normal routine as possible. He should continue to have his meals at the same time every day. And he should have an opportunity to exercise. After a few hours in the car, your dog may have a great deal of pent-up energy. Once it is spent, he may be more inclined to ride quietly. And he will enjoy it more.

There are some important items that you should take with you. Always carry both food and water for your pet. Unless you know that you will be able to buy additional food, you should bring enough for the entire trip. If you feed your dog canned food, remember to pack a can opener.

Including a jug of water from home will ensure that your pet gets enough liquids. He may refuse to drink strange-tasting water; this could lead to dehydration. You can help your dog adjust by mixing a small amount of water from home with the new water. In a short period of time, your pet should get used to the taste.

In addition to his own food and water, a travelling pet needs a collar or harness and an unbreakable leash. Besides a rabies tag, the collar or harness should have an identification tag traceable to someone who can rescue the animal. If your dog gets lost on vacation and only your home number is on the tag, you will not be there to answer the phone. Before departing on your trip, you may want to change the regular ID tag for one that has the number of a friend or relative who will be able to contact you at all times.

Another item that you should take with you is a health certificate, proving that your dog is current on all vaccinations. For good measure, you might include his favorite blanket and a few toys. You also need some small plastic bags and twist ties. They should be used to clean up after your dog at rest stops and in parks.

It is a good idea to put all of his supplies into a carrying case. Then, you can easily keep track of all of the animal's provisions. This will make it easier to tend to your dog at rest stops and overnight layovers. If you want, you can purchase a carrying case that comes packed with bowls and supplies.

If the drive is only a few hours in duration, you will not have to worry about your pet becoming too thirsty in the car. A trip longer than that will require that your animal have access to water. Make frequent stops so that your dog can get a drink. Or, you might want to fill a weighted bowl full of ice. The weight will keep the bowl from tipping over. Having the water in ice form will keep it from making a mess of your car. Hopefully, by the time it melts, your dog will have drunk enough so that the remaining water does not slosh out of the bowl. You can also purchase special travel water bowls that are designed to catch any water before it can spill out.

When packing the car, you must make some special arrangements if your dog will be riding in a crate. Make sure that the suitcases placed in back do not restrict the air circulation for your pet. You can put the water bowl, blanket and a toy or two in the crate. Hopefully, once the dog is situated, you still have room for the rest of your family.

Finally, as you cruise down the highway, you should keep the air conditioner on or a window open. Every couple of hours, you should stop to let the dog stretch his legs, play for a few minutes and relieve himself. A rest stop will be a very unfamiliar place; even a dog that normally does not leave your side may get spooked and run away. You should keep your pet on a leash and restrict him to the area where dogs are allowed. And be sure to clean up after him.

Vacationing With Your Dog

The key to a good vacation with your dog is planning. You should always call ahead to your destination to make sure that your pet is as welcome as you are. Do not assume that a park or campground will let animals in, even if they are confined to leashes. In fact, you are more likely to get your dog into a hotel than a state or national park.

Many hotels do not allow any small animals inside. Others, however, simply charge a security deposit; some even have kennels. You should verify a hotel's animal policy before starting your trip. You do not want to arrive after a long day and discover that you cannot find accommodations.

When checking in, ask to speak with the manager. Introduce him to your pet and show him the crate that you will use to confine the animal. Besides agreeing to pay a security deposit, suggest that the manager examine the room with you before checking out the next day. This protects you from unwarranted charges being added to your bill. And it works well if you are trying to establish a relationship with the hotel. Oftentimes, your next visit will be much easier. And whenever you leave your dog alone in a hotel room, put him in his crate. This keeps him from damaging the room or escaping if a hotel employee opens your door.

If your vacation will keep you in one location, you may want to consider renting a house rather than staying in a hotel. You still have to adhere to all local laws concerning pets. But you do not have to worry about disturbing the guests next door or scaring a maid coming in to clean your room.

If you want to get out of the city, backpacking is a good vacation to take with your dog. Some larger dogs can be trained to carry a pack, so they can lug their own food and water. You need to make sure that your camp site will allow pets.

Another possibility is to rent a recreational vehicle. An RV is large enough that your dog will have enough room inside to stretch his legs. And with that much space for packing, you may be able to take along a portable dog run. This will give your dog added room to exercise when you stop for the night. Also, you can confine your dog in the mobile home on those nights when you opt to stay in a hotel. However, you must be sure that it is not too hot outside and your pet has adequate ventilation. An RV is just like a very large car; a dog left inside can overheat and suffer heatstroke.

If you plan well enough, you may be able to find

a good boarding kennel in each town you are planning to visit. That way, if you stay for a day or so with a relative who does not like animals, you can board your dog while you are there. Then you can pick him up when you resume your travels. (Since most kennels require residents to be current on their vaccinations, be sure to get a health certificate from your veterinarian before leaving home.)

If you are planning to take your dog abroad, check with the embassy or a consulate of each country that you are going to visit. Many countries have strict health restrictions regarding animals. Several require that all animals be quarantined for a period of time upon arrival. This period often ranges from four weeks to six months. It makes no sense to take your dog on a two week vacation if he would be locked up for a month before he could join you. Unless you will be out of the country for an extended period of time, you should leave your dog at home.

Before embarking on a vacation with your dog, you may want to contact a travel agent or service. A travel professional will help you organize your thoughts as well as give you additional ideas and tips. That will ensure that your trip will be enjoyable for everybody, including the family pet.

Travelling By Air

Flying can be a good way to travel for a dog. It takes less time than driving, so your dog will spend less time being confined. But there are dangers. In order to make your dog's trip as safe as possible, you need to plan your trip carefully and well in advance.

The initial step is to determine whether your dog can withstand the rigors of airline travel. For a dog, airline travel is extremely stressful. The animal is isolated in unfamiliar surroundings. The baggage compartment of many planes is not always pressurized at the same level as the passenger cabin. In most cases, the flow of air is limited. The compartments can be very hot and stuffy. In addition, there might be other items in the shipping area compounding your dog's problems. Dry ice, a frequent packing material for perishable goods, produces vapors that can be toxic to a dog.

Before you take your dog on a plane, he should be examined by your veterinarian. Since stress forces the body to work harder, your dog should be in very good health. Puppies, older dogs and dogs that are ill probably should not make the trip. Also, breeds that typically have breathing problems, such as flat-faced dogs, are better off left at home.

Once your veterinarian clears your dog, you can select an airline. You should learn about the animal policy of each airline that flies to your destination. While the transport of animals on all airlines is governed by the U.S. Department of Agriculture, each carrier has its own regulations. The policies vary widely. Some charge you a shipping fee; others do not as long as you accompany the dog on the flight. Most airlines require you to produce a current health certificate.

A few airlines allow dogs on board with passengers if the animals can fit into a crate small enough to go under a seat. However, most require that dogs travel in a special carrier that is placed in the cargo compartment. There may also be a size restriction. After comparing the various regulations, you can select the carrier that best suits your needs.

The next step is setting up the itinerary. If possible, pick a nonstop flight. Many of the problems that crop up for dogs in transit occur while changing planes. Your pet may have to sit out on a tarmac in the rain or hot sun while waiting to be placed on the next plane. If you have to make connections, see if you can claim your dog between flights. You could then let him out of the crate for a few minutes.

The most dreaded problem is that cargo can be misplaced. It is possible for your dog to end up on the wrong plane or to be simply lost. While the chance of recovery is high, the amount of stress for your pet and you will increase. In addition, the time needed to complete the journey will lengthen considerably. What was going to be a four-hour confinement in a carrier could become a ten- or twelve-hour ordeal. If you do not have to make any stops or change planes, the potential for a disastrous problem decreases greatly.

Also, you should try to fly at off-peak times. Avoid the warmer parts of the day. The luggage compartment of a plane can become very hot. While the temperature in the cargo hold is regulated when the engines are running, it is not when the plane is sitting at the gate. While waiting for the plane to taxi for take-off, your dog may dehydrate and overheat. His situation will be more serious if he is scared and stressed out. An anxious dog pants; this compounds his efforts to regulate his body temperature and contributes to dehydration. The possibility of heat-stroke increases significantly. Travelling in the cool of the early morning or late evening is much safer.

In addition to being cooler, off-peak times have another advantage. They are usually less crowded. Less people means less luggage to be handled. Your dog will probably be moved on and off the plane faster. He will probably get more attention from the handlers, as well.

Even if you can book a nonstop flight at an off-peak time, flying during a holiday period is a bad idea. All flights will be crowded. This usually means having to check your dog earlier and wait longer for him when you arrive at your destination. This will add an extra hour or two to the time that your pet is confined in a carrier. In addition, airlines are often delayed during holidays. If your flight is late departing, the length of time that your dog sits in a hot, stuffy cargo hold may increase.

After weighing all of the factors, you should be able to select a flight. When making your reservation, be sure to make one for your dog, as well. You do not want to show up at the airport with a non-refundable ticket and find out that there is no room for your pet.

The next step is to prepare for the trip. Whether your dog rides in the passenger or luggage compartment, he will need a sturdy carrier. Many airlines have crates available for sale; some require that you purchase one from them. If you have a choice, you can also find suitable carriers at a pet store or in a catalog. Check with the airline to find out the size specifications as well as any other requirements that apply.

The crate should be large enough for your pet to stand up, turn around and lie down. It should be made of plastic or other material that is strong enough to withstand a heavy blow. This helps protect your dog in case of a shipping accident. The interior should be smooth and rust-free. There should be plenty of openings to allow adequate airflow. An outside rim should keep the openings from being blocked when other luggage is placed next to the crate.

Before starting out on the journey, make sure that your dog has on an identification tag. Also, you should label the crate clearly with your name, your dog's name, your destination and a phone number there. It is a good idea to include the name and number of somebody back home; that way, a concerned party can be contacted about your pet if you are unreachable. Also, you should tie a leash to the outside. This gives the airline personnel a means to restrain your pet if, for some reason, he has to be taken out of the crate.

An airline usually requires that you check in an hour or two before your departure. Follow the animal as far through the system as possible. Ask if your dog can be left with you until the plane boards. However, your pet may be better off if you leave him as soon as he goes in the crate. Some dogs become very upset if they are caged while their owners are nearby. Naturally, they would prefer to be with their loved ones rather than be locked up. Yet once the owners are out of sight, the animals often calm down and go to sleep.

Also, while checking in, request that your dog's crate be put on the plane as late as possible. The last bag on is often the first one off.

Motion Sickness and Fear of Travelling

Whether you travel by car or by plane, your dog may suffer from motion sickness. Motion sickness is caused by the constant rocking of the inner ear organs that aid in balancing. When they are out of kilter, they send a signal to the brain, which in turn tells the body that something is wrong.

Besides motion sickness, your dog may be so scared of the sights and sounds of travelling that he makes himself sick. A dog under an excessive amount of stress often trembles and has high pulse and respiratory rates. Your dog may hyperventilate, vomit or have diarrhea.

To minimize the problem, you should avoid giving your dog any food on the day of the trip. This may prevent the animal from developing an upset stomach. A healthy dog should be able to get by just fine on an empty stomach if the trip is less than twelve hours long. Younger or older dogs may be able to go four to eight hours without eating their normal meal.

Your pet should be able to drink as much water as he wants until an hour or so before the trip. If you are travelling by car, you can take the additional steps of making frequent stops for water and exercise and keeping the car well-ventilated with air conditioning or open windows. On extremely long flights, try to give your dog some water whenever changing planes. If nothing else, allow him to drink as soon as you arrive at your destination.

If your pet has a chronic problem with travelling, your veterinarian may be able to help you. Medications to control motion sickness work about as well for dogs as they do for people. Your doctor may be able to recommend some over-the-counter medications that will control your pet's illness. He can also tell you how to safely use them. The amount and frequency of the dosage will be determined by the weight of your pet and the length of the trip.

If your pet's sickness is due to fear, a tranquilizer may be a good idea. It will probably make your dog very sleepy and a little disoriented; the animal will not know what is going on around him. Sometimes, a tranquilizer can also help with motion sickness.

But its usage can be tricky. The correct dose is

not the same for every animal in every circumstance. You can easily underdose or overdose your dog. Once the drug has been given, you can expect your pet to be groggy for at least eight hours, if not an entire day. You should be judicious in its use. It does not make sense to give a dog a pill that will last for twenty-four hours if the car trip is only thirty minutes long.

Also, a drug can have several side effects. Most dogs on tranquilizers get a dry mouth and red eyes. Ill animals can become sicker. Other dogs experience a reverse response to the tranquilizers; they become agitated and aggressive instead of calm and docile.

One other factor should be considered when contemplating tranquilizing a dog before going on an airplane. The drug reduces your pet's responses to all outside stimuli. While the tranquilizer makes the animal more docile, it also diminishes his capability to regulate his body temperature. Given the temperature extremes that can occur in a luggage compartment, a tranquilized dog has a much greater risk of heatstroke.

If you are contemplating the use of a tranquilizer, discuss this in advance with your veterinarian. You may want to try a test dose several days prior to the trip. Then you will find out how the medication affects your pet.

Chapter Twelve
Leaving Your Dog Behind

There will be times when you go on vacation and are not be able to take your pet with you. If your pet were a cat, you might be able to leave her alone in the house for a couple of days without any problems. This is assuming, of course, that the feline would have plenty of food and water to satisfy her needs. A canine, on the other hand, is not so maintenance-free. You will have to make arrangements for your dog to receive his normal, proper care while you are gone.

Pet Sitters

The best solution is to find a pet sitter. This is a person who will come into your house and take care of the pet chores. This scenario has a couple of advantages for your dog. First, this will enable your dog to remain in his home environment. He will feel more secure, since he will not have to worry about being in unfamiliar territory. He will still have his favorite spot to lie down in and know where to get water. Second, a pet sitter can keep your dog on his normal schedule. The sitter can plan her visits to coincide with the usual times that your dog is fed and exercised.

A pet sitter can be advantageous for you, as well.

You may be able to find a sitter who will stay in your house while you are gone. This will keep the place occupied, reducing the chance of a burglary.

Pet sitters need exactly the same kind of information that a human baby sitter would need. You should compile a written list of your pet's activities and routines. For example, note the exact amounts and times of feeding. Jot down exactly when and where the animal is walked. And be sure that the sitter knows when and how to give heartworm medicine. Do not assume that your sitter will remember all of your verbal requests or know how your various pets are treated. Leave the phone number where you can be reached and the number of your veterinarian. These are essential in case of an emergency.

If you have the chance, reinforce your instructions by actually showing the sitter how to perform some of the tasks. You may have a particular way of grooming your dog. Your pet might be used to a set order when it comes to activities such as feeding, exercising and playing. There is a big difference between reading about the nuances of your dog's care and witnessing how the jobs are performed. Walking your sitter through the steps will guarantee that the caretaker will know what to do on a daily basis.

If possible, the sitter should be someone that your dog already knows and trusts. However, if the person is a new acquaintance, your dog should meet the sitter before you leave town. This is a good idea for both the sitter and the dog. You might be able to determine if there are any personality conflicts before a problem erupts.

Just before leaving, check the supplies of food, vitamins, rawhide and treats. If you are running low on any, either replenish the stock or leave enough money for your sitter to do so. If your sitter will be buying supplies, write down the names of the correct brands. Also, verify that your dog is wearing proper identification. And lastly, make sure that your sitter can get into the house. It is not uncommon for people to cover every detail to ensure the safe and proper care of their dog except one: they forget to give the sitter a key.

Even though your dog stays in his home environment, he can still have problems. Most pet sitters do not stay with the dog during the night. They typically feed and exercise the animal at the appropriate time but then go home. Your dog may be used to being by himself during the day while you are at work but he usually has companionship at night. If you have more than one pet, the two animals can keep each other company. But if your dog is all by himself, he may become scared or lonely.

This anxiety can lead to unusual behavioral responses, such as a loss of housebreaking skills or destructive chewing episodes. To counter this, you might ask your sitter to spend a couple of evenings in your house, watching TV, reading or whatever. The sitter might not even have to play with the dog; simply being in the house may be enough. If you plan to frequently leave your dog alone at night, take steps to adjust him to your absence. These are covered in the chapter on separation anxiety (see page 170).

Other "At Home" Options

A variation of having someone come into your home is taking your dog to a friend's home. Although your pet will no longer be in the safety of his own territory, he will at least be in a "homey" environment where his caretaker is there all night. This set-up works well if you are planning a trip that is longer than a few days. The person caring for your dog will not have to make trips to your house every day.

It is best if your pet knows and trusts the person with whom he will be staying. Ideally, he will also be familiar with the home where he will go. If he is not, you may want to take him over for a visit before your planned trip. This gives him an opportunity to get his bearings and meet the inhabitants. It also gives you a chance to see if the dog is comfortable in that setting. If so, then you will have more confidence that he can cope well in your absence.

When going to stay at another house, your dog should take a few items with him. He will need a supply of food, his food bowl, a leash and a collar with proper identification tags. You should also send a couple of items from home that he enjoys having with him. A favorite blanket or toy will give him some extra security. Be sure to leave the name and number of your veterinarian as well as copies of the animal's health and vaccination certificates. You should also give the caretaker the name a good kennel, just in case something comes up that cuts short your dog's stay.

It is asking a lot of someone to be responsible for

another creature. If you are going to be away for a few days, a friend may be willing to care for your pet for free. However, it is not fair to expect somebody to take care of your dog for more than a week.

If you are going to be gone for an extended period of time, you might consider a commercial pet sitting service. These usually charge by the number of animals and the number of visits required to care for them. Two cats requiring one trip a day may be cheaper than one dog needing two or three visits a day. When evaluating a service, make sure that it is licensed, registered and bonded. You should also ask for recommendations and check references. After selecting one, be certain that the staff can get hold of you in case of an emergency. You should also leave the name and number of your veterinarian and of a friend who is authorized to make decisions for you, if you are unreachable.

Boarding Kennels

If you cannot find someone to stay with your dog or no one is willing to take him while you are gone, you will have to put him in a boarding kennel. While there are documented cases of boarded pets not being fed or exercised, most kennels will take good care of your dog. However, some are better than others. You just need to know how to find them.

First, the best sources of information are your veterinarian and your friends. Your veterinary clinic may even have facilities to board your dog. This would have an added advantage. Not only would your pet get excellent care while you are out of town, he would already be at the hospital should any emergency arise. If the clinic cannot take your dog, your veterinarian will be able to recommend a few reputable kennels. Also, ask your friends which kennels they have used and what sort of experiences they have had. A further resource is the American Boarding Kennel Association in Colorado Springs, Colorado; they can give you a list of the certified kennels in your area.

Call each kennel to get an idea of price, hours and amenities. Make sure that runs are available for adequate exercise. Some facilities only have cages. This is not appropriate for a dog unless the animal is walked several times a day. Most dogs do best with an indoor/outdoor run set-up.

After narrowing down your choices to a few facilities, visit each one. (If a kennel refuses visits or will not let you see the cages and runs, cross it off your list.) Make sure that the cages are big enough for your dog to stand up, turn around and lie down comfortably. The runs should be large enough so that your pet can get adequate exercise. Both the cages and the runs should be clean and in good repair; none should show signs of rust or extensive wear.

The kennel area should have good ventilation. This helps keep your dog cool in the summer. Proper air circulation also reduces the chance of any contagious diseases spreading from one animal to the next. The entire area should smell good; a building with a foul odor is usually harboring germs.

In addition, take notice of the dogs being boarded.

They should appear to be alert, well-fed, watered and cared for just as you would want your dog to be.

The kennel staff should be courteous to you and gentle with the animals. They should know the names and special requirements of the pets boarding with them. Be sure to ask lots of questions. Find out if someone is on duty twenty-four hours a day. This is important if an emergency situation arises during the night, requiring that the animals be taken out of the building. Ask whether there is a veterinarian associated with the kennel or if the staff would be able to transport your pet to your own veterinarian in an emergency. Make sure that the staff will be able to provide your pet with a special diet or medication, if needed. A good bonus is a kennel that has an area to isolate a pet if he does get sick; this reduces the chance of the other animals being exposed.

Inquire about any special policies that the kennel may have. Many require that each dog be bathed before going home. Also, most will bathe and dip a dog that shows any signs of external parasites; the owner would be required to pay for the service. This is a good policy. One dog with fleas or mites could infest the entire kennel if the animal were not treated immediately. Since the owners are out of town, contacting them for authorization may be impossible.

If you have two dogs that get along, see if the kennel will allow them to stay in the same run. If they are good buddies, they will be able to keep each other company. This will reduce the stress of being in a strange environment.

Last, find out if the kennel has any extra services

available for your pet. Many have programs where your dog can be taken out for exercise each day. Others have elaborate accommodations that give your dog his own bed, toys and the other amenities of home. Some even offer swimming programs or provide your dog with his own wading pool. After inspecting and evaluating all the kennels on your list, you should be able to pick the one that is best for your dog.

Once you have made your decision, discuss all arrangements well in advance. This keeps problems from cropping up when you drop your pet off. Write down all the important information about your dog. List what and when he should be fed. If the kennel does not have the brand of food that you desire, supply your own. Find out exactly what health certificates and vaccinations are required. Agree in advance to any grooming, bathing or other services that you want performed. For an emergency, leave a number where you can be reached and the number of your veterinarian. Ask if you can bring a favorite toy or blanket to help relieve the homesickness. And learn what hours and days the kennel is open to pick up your pet when you return home.

And most importantly, find out the latest time that the kennel will accept your dog on the day of drop-off. All your preplanning will go for naught if the kennel closes before you get there. The key to a happy boarding experience is to communicate and plan well in advance.

If your dog has never been to a kennel before, his first stay should be for no more than a couple of days.

It is a good idea to weigh him before he goes in and as soon as he comes out. If he maintains his weight, you can assume that he did fairly well. Once he has had a successful stay, you can increase the length of time that he boards.

Vaccinations Needed By a Boarded Dog

When it comes to viral and bacterial infections, dogs in a kennel are similar to children in a classroom; they are confined in places with restricted ventilation. If one animal has a virus, virtually every other dog in the kennel will be exposed. To protect your dog while he is boarding, you should check to see if he is up to date on his shots. In fact, most kennels will not accept your dog unless you have written verification that all of his vaccinations are current. Besides the usual annual vaccinations, your dog should receive two additional vaccines that will help stave off common diseases associated with boarding dogs.

The first of these is the bordetella vaccine; it helps prevent a disease called kennel cough. Kennel cough is a highly contagious respiratory infection that occurs frequently whenever dogs are brought together as a group. The illness effects the throat, windpipe and smaller airways to the lungs. After contracting kennel cough, a dog may initially show respiratory signs. Or, he may act depressed, quiet and tired. He may also vomit and have diarrhea. As the illness progresses, the animal's initial signs usually disappear. He then develops chronic bronchitis. At this point, a very noticeable sign that something is wrong is a dry, harsh cough. The dog will sound somewhat like a honking goose.

For adult dogs, kennel cough is usually not life-threatening. Most cases subside over a period of several weeks. In some cases, however, the illness can result in pneumonia. Therefore, a trip to your veterinary clinic is recommended. The veterinarian can prescribe antibiotics to fight the infection and additional medicine to give your dog some relief from the cough.

For some dogs and most puppies, the disease can be much more serious. They may get so congested that they have trouble breathing. Some animals have even died from complications related to kennel cough. Puppies and animals with serious symptoms must be treated by a veterinarian.

The other illness commonly contracted at kennels is gastroenteritis. Dogs with gastroenteritis have inflammation of the digestive tract. One virus known to cause the illness is parvo virus. It is a common virus, so a vaccination for parvo is part of the recommended annual inoculations for your dog.

Another viral cause of gastroenteritis is canine corona virus. It is not as common as parvo, but it can be prevalent in a boarding kennel. The corona virus attacks the lining of the dog's stomach and intestines, causing vomiting and diarrhea. The disease can last for weeks and is often fatal, especially in puppies.

A new vaccine has been developed to prevent corona virus. If your dog is going to be in a kennel, he should be protected. The vaccine is available alone or in combination with your dog's other vaccinations.

Check with your veterinarian if you are unsure when to update your dog's inoculations. Most are given on an annual basis. However, some vaccinations, such as the bordetella and parvo vaccines, may be given as often as every six months. The frequency depends upon the prevalent diseases in your area.

Chapter Thirteen
The Fourth of July

The Fourth of July is the best holiday of the summer but it can be difficult for your dog. With your help, he will enjoy the holiday picnic. Provide him with plenty of shade and water to prevent overheating and dehydration. And make sure that he does not gorge himself on hotdogs, potato salad, baked beans and marshmallows. (The dangers of overeating are outlined in the chapter on Thanksgiving, see page 189.) If you do bring your dog to the Fourth of July festivities, treat him as you would a child. Let him have fun, but keep him out of trouble.

The Danger of Fireworks

Even though your dog may love the picnic, he should be left at home during the fireworks display. The explosions of sound, light and color can be terrifying to a dog. A frightened, anxious animal may lose his normal inhibitions and behave irrationally. If he tries to escape from the ruckus, he may dart out into a street and get hit by a car. And he might overreact to actions that would not usually bother him. For instance, on a normal occasion, your dog might not mind his ears or tail being pulled by a child. But when frightened, the animal may perceive the child's action as a physical threat. If your dog responds in an aggressive manner, the child could end up being knocked down or bitten.

On the other hand, if the fireworks do not scare your pet, he may want to play with them. An excited dog might chase the flying, burning objects. If he has the opportunity, he may pick up a lighted firecracker in his mouth. Undoubtedly, he will be injured. At best, he will suffer a slight burn. The outcome could easily be much worse.

Protecting Your Dog From Fireworks

If your dog is going to be exposed to fireworks, you should keep him on a leash. That way, you will be able to control him if he overreacts. In all likelihood, however, he will be better off at home.

Even the safety of your house may not shield your dog from the effects of fireworks. While they cannot physically harm him, the noise can still be frightening. The best thing that you can do is to be there with him, holding or distracting him until his fear subsides. This will keep him from damaging anything in your house, including himself.

However, if you want to go to the fireworks show, your dog may have to spend the time alone. You might be reluctant to let him have free reign in the house while you are gone. An animal attempting to escape or hide from the loud noises may hurt himself or his surroundings. Behavioral responses often range from the loss of housebreaking skills to destructive chewing. In addition, extremely anxious dogs have been known to claw through wooden doors and put holes in the floor.

Leaving your dog in the backyard will safeguard the house but will not protect the animal. In his frantic state, he may run without regard for his safety. He can easily slam into a fence or fall over an immovable object. He may also get loose and run away. He is especially at risk if he is tethered. A frightened animal should never be tied; his leash or chain can catch on something and choke him.

Your dog should be inside during a fireworks display. Both your pet and the house can be kept safe by confining the animal. If he has a kennel, he will be comfortable there. Since the crate is his den, he will feel safer there than anywhere else. If the crate is wire mesh, cover the top and sides with a blanket.

However, if you do not own a crate, you should confine your dog in a relatively small area where he is safe and cannot cause damage. Leave him a place to hide; he may want to crawl under a bed, into a closet or under a blanket. You should also remove anything that the dog can break or knock over. If you are going to be gone for only an hour or so, do not give him any water in his hiding place. This will reduce the chance of an accident inside the house. And you can leave a radio on. Even if the music does not soothe him, it will help drown out the noise of the fireworks.

If you know that your dog will be truly terrified by the fireworks, you might consider giving the animal a tranquilizer. This will allow him to remain calm through the show, but there are drawbacks. First, the medication must be given at least an hour before the fireworks start in order to be effective. If not, your pet will be terrified during the show and then become very sedate an hour later. Second, there is no such thing as a one-hour tranquilizer. Your pet will be under the influence of the medication for twelve to twenty-four hours. But if the options are either to tranquilize the dog or to subject your house and pet to major damage, the animal is better off medicated.

Before giving any tranquilizers to your dog, discuss the situation with your veterinarian. The doctor is in the best position to point out the risks and benefits for your pet. He may also have some other solutions that are just as effective and much safer.

Chapter Fourteen
At the Beach

A day at the beach is a wonderful way to spend free time during the summer. Having your dog with you can add to your enjoyment and be great fun for your pet, as well. But the sand and water do pose a few hazards that you should be aware of. With a little bit of pre-planning, however, the hindrances to a perfect day can be easily avoided.

What To Keep In Mind

First of all, remember that not all animals are natural swimmers. Dogs usually enjoy a dip in the ocean, but you must make sure that your pet can swim before he goes in the water. The ocean is not the place to learn to swim. Even a dog that is an accomplished swimmer may be scared on his first visit to the sea. The waves can knock your dog under the water; an undertow can pull him away from the beach and disorient him. If he has a bad experience, your dog may not ever want to go back in.

And the creatures of the water can harm him. Your dog can just as easily be stung by jelly fish or pinched by crabs as you can. These stings and pinches are as painful for him as they are for you. Your dog may actually be more at risk; if his curiosity is peaked, he may not retreat from a creature that could harm him.

There is a good rule of thumb to follow at the beach. If you are not willing to go in the water, you should keep your dog out, as well. Just because he has four legs does not mean that he is better equipped than you to handle the ocean.

On his first trip to the beach, your dog should be introduced gradually to running on sand. Soft sand is a great place to run only if your legs are in good shape. Dogs that are out of shape or overweight can pull ligaments and tendons just like people do.

When you first arrive, let him run only on the hard-packed sand along the water's edge. As he becomes accustomed to the loose footing, he should be able to venture onto the soft sand. However, when you are on deep, loose sand, you should refrain from playing games that will require your dog to run, jump or turn suddenly. There is a chance that he will hurt muscles or joints while playing in the deep sand. Save running and playing in loose sand for future trips to the beach. By then, your dog will have adjusted to moving through the sand.

The sun and heat can take their toll on your dog. Remember that he will overheat before you do. You should bring some sort of shelter for your dog. A large umbrella can provide enough shade for both your pet and you. You should also bring fresh water for your dog to drink. He should not be allowed to drink sea water. It has too much saline and will make him sick.

You can provide additional comfort by giving your dog a means of getting off the sand. The sand reflects the sun and can hold heat. A towel or blanket will keep your dog cooler. It will also prevent the insects that live in the sand from crawling on your pet. This helps prevent itchy bites and skin inflammation.

At the End of the Day

Once the day is over, you should rinse off your dog. After running, swimming and lounging all day, he will undoubtedly be covered with salt, sand and dirt. These remove the natural oils in the coat and make your dog's skin susceptible to skin infections. In addition, the sand itself is irritating. After it works through the hair and down to the skin, the sand will rub your dog as he moves. This abrasive action can create sores and cause itching, which can lead to self-mutilation and hot spots.

Rinsing the dog is not a taxing chore. Your dog will not need a full-fledged grooming bath, complete with shampoo and conditioner. A plain-water rinse with a hose or shower is sufficient. And the animal probably will not object. Most dogs that like the beach and water enjoy being hosed off.

Your dog will have a good time at the beach. But remember that, at the end of the day, he will feel just like you do. He will be hot, tired, sticky and thirsty. After he has been rinsed off, his perfect day can be concluded with some fresh water to drink and a little rest.

Boating With Your Dog

Dogs always prefer to be with their owners. So if you like to go sailing or boating, your dog will want to go, too. Your dog can have a wonderful time on the water, but you should take some precautions to ensure his safety.

First, he should wear a lifevest. These are available in many pet stores and catalogs. Even a strong swimmer can get in trouble if he does go overboard. It is much harder to get a dog back into a boat than a person; your pet can tire and drown while you are trying to rescue him. A lifevest will buoy him up until you can get to him. In addition, you should never tie the animal to the boat. If it capsizes, your pet may be drowned.

Before taking your dog on the water with you, you should experiment to see how he does. On his first visit to your boat, you should let him get on the craft but leave it moored to the dock. After he has familiarized himself with the surroundings, you can take him out for a short trip. Ideally, the sea should be calm so the amount of pitch will be minimal. As your dog becomes accustomed to the boat's movements, he will be ready for longer excursions. If you plan to spend hours on the water, be sure to bring potable water for drinking and provide your pet with a place to relieve himself. Once your pet is situated, you will be set for smooth sailing ahead.

Chapter Fifteen
A Lost Dog

Since your dog will probably be spending a great deal of time outside during the summer, the chance of him getting lost will increase. Having a lost pet is one of the most frightening experiences that any dog owner will ever encounter. One moment, all is well. The next, the animal jumps a fence or runs out the front door and is gone. You drive up and down the block feverishly looking for him. After several hours, you reluctantly call off your search. You return home, distraught at the thought that your beloved dog is still out there, hungry and scared. You have to wait at home until you can resume your search, hoping for the best but expecting the worst.

Unfortunately, this scenario is quite common. Well over 2 million pets are lost annually in the United States. Many are never returned to their owners. You should do what you can to keep this tragedy from happening to your dog and you.

Act Before Your Dog Disappears

The best way to increase the chance of finding your dog is to take action before he is lost. The first step is to make sure that your dog wears a sturdy collar. Those made of leather or nylon are good. (Choke collars are not; they are training devices.) Many collars have safety strips that reflect light. This makes it easier to see your dog after dark. It gives you a better chance of finding him. The collar could also prevent him from being hit by a car.

The collar should fit snugly but not too tightly; you should be able to fit three fingers underneath it. The buckle should be smooth and work easily. Check your dog's collar frequently to make sure that it has not worn out or stretched too much; replace it as needed. And most importantly, your dog should wear it at all times. You never know when your pet may slip away and get lost. The collar will not help him if it sits in your kitchen while your pet is out.

The collar should have three tags on it that help identify your dog. The first has your dog's name, your name and your address and phone number. Make sure that you change this tag every time that you move. You might also consider using a tracking agency. An organization such as this will furnish you with a tag that has an ID number for your dog and a toll-free phone number on it. If a person finds your pet, he can trace the animal back to you by calling the agency. This allows you to leave the same tag on your pet if you move. But you still have to notify the tracking agency of each address and phone change.

The second tag is a local license. Most communities require that all dogs be registered. Compliance is a good idea. Besides keeping you from being fined, it can save your dog's life. If he is not wearing this tag, your dog may be considered a stray. Stray animals are often euthanized at shelters after a few days. In addition, the registration number on the license can be used to trace your dog back to you.

The third tag is a rabies tag. These are issued by your veterinarian and show that your dog is vaccinated against rabies. A rabies tag has the expiration date of the vaccination as well as the name, address and phone number of your veterinary clinic. Your pet can be traced back to you through the hospital.

Besides being a third source of identification, a rabies tag will also protect your dog from euthanasia. If your pet is loose and bites someone, he will be destroyed as a potential rabies carrier unless it can be shown that he has a current rabies vaccination. The rabies tag may save his life if he is picked up as a stray and you are not there to identify him.

While tags are the best the best way to identify a lost dog, they do have one drawback; they occasionally fall off. The collar itself may be the only identification left on your dog if he wanders away. So, it is a good idea to purchase a collar that has your dog's name and your phone number imprinted directly on it.

Besides putting a sturdy collar and the proper tags on your pet, you should have several up-to-date color photos of your dog. It is difficult to give someone enough detail verbally so that he can identify your pet. Many people mistakenly believe that all dogs of a particular breed look alike. And there are different definitions for the same color; your idea of red may be somebody else's idea of brown. A color photo will keep you both in sync. In addition, a photo will point out any important characteristics that you may have forgotten. Seeing a tuft of white hair on the chest or an ear may make the difference between your dog being lost or found.

The photos should be taken from the top, front, back and both sides of the animal. Update them every six months. Over the course of his life, your dog's physical appearance changes. His coat may become darker; he may experience some hair loss; he may gain weight. Current photos will reflect these changes. You cannot count on a five-year-old picture to adequately identify your dog to someone who has never seen him before.

You should keep all of the information regarding your pet in a file. This will give you quick access to all of the registration numbers, health certificates and photographs. Also, keep the photo negatives in the file; you will want to have many prints made to hand out and need a picture to put on your "lost dog" posters. The file should be placed in a secure spot where you can easily find it. In a time of crisis, you do not want to waste time searching for crucial documents. The time would be better spent searching for your dog.

Other Forms of Identification

All of the steps discussed so far are good, but they are not perfect. As mentioned before, tags and collars can slip off. Your photos may clearly identify unique markings, but they have to be shown to somebody who has seen the animal.

There are other good methods of pet identification that are more permanent. One is having your dog tattooed. A dog tattoo is a series of numbers printed on the animal's inner thigh. The procedure is performed by a veterinarian or another skilled individual. The number inked onto your pet is your choice. Most people use either their social security or driver's license number. The number can then be sent to a national registry. If a shelter (or anyone who finds a lost dog) calls the registry with the tattoo number, the animal can be traced back to you.

Unfortunately, there is not a standardized numbering system for pets. And there are several registering agencies. So, anyone finding your dog would have to call the right registry in order to reunite the pet with the owner.

Having your dog tattooed is a good idea, anyway. The staff at animal shelters routinely look for tattoos on lost animals. If a dog has one, the assumption is that he is somebody's pet. That may save him from being destroyed or sold to a research institute.

The latest in pet identification comes from California. In some locations, pets can be fitted with a microchip that contains a code number. The chip is inserted under the skin; it cannot be lost or removed. Lost pets can be scanned and their identifying code numbers traced to their owners. This system is relatively inexpensive, permanent and effective. It is rapidly gaining in popularity.

What To Do If Your Dog Is Lost

If your dog does become lost, immediate action will increase your chances of finding him. First, file a missing animal report with all of the animal shelters and humane societies in your area. When filling out forms, attach a copy of one of the photos.

Next, spread the word. The more people that know your pet is lost, the better are your chances of finding him. Advertise in your local newspapers. Give a description of your dog, listing the breed, color, sex, size and weight. Emphasize any unusual features. State when and where he was last seen. Offer a reward. (It is a good idea not to give the amount. If you offer too much, a lot of quacks will call; if you offer too little, some may think that it is not worth the effort.) Also, give your telephone number only. For security purposes, you should not include your name and address.

Print large, easy-to-read flyers. It is very important that the flyers have a photo on them. Also, include all of the information that was used in the newspaper ad. The flyers should be posted throughout the area and in as many of the surrounding localities as possible.

Tell your letter carrier and the neighborhood children to be on the lookout. You should also contact the local veterinary clinics; inform them that you will be responsible for any fees if your dog is brought to the hospital and requires medical treatment.

Call the animal shelters daily and visit all of them frequently. They can be very hectic places; your dog might be there without the staff realizing it. Find out what each facility's policy is on euthanizing animals. If one shelter destroys an animal after its fifth day there, you should stop by that facility every third or fourth day. That will ensure that your dog will not be euthanized inadvertently. Also, contact the shelters of surrounding communities; it is surprising how far a dog can travel in a short period of time.

And lastly, do not give up. The key to finding a lost pet is perseverance. Search your area every day, calling your dog's name and talking with people. There have been cases where pets have been found several weeks or months after being lost.

Part III

Fall

Chapter Sixteen
Fall Basics

The transition from summer to fall has a tremendous impact on your dog. The days will be getting cooler and drier, as well as shorter. These changes can affect his health and behavior.

Fall Activities

Fall can be a great time for your dog. Annoying insects such as mosquitoes and flies are starting to decrease. The weather is cooler, crisper and less humid than in the summer. Dogs that hate the heat get new energy and vitality as the mercury falls. You should take advantage of your dog's renewed vigor and get him outside as often as possible. If your pet has not been very active over the summer, he will be out of shape. The cool of the fall gives him a chance to get back into good physical condition before the cold of winter sets in.

You should be extra cautious for the first few sessions outside. A dog that has been lazy during the hot weather will be very excited to be outdoors and playing again. He can overexert himself. You can help him help himself by starting with short strolls for the first week or so. These should last no longer than ten to fifteen minutes. Gradually increase the length and speed of the walks as the animal grows stronger and more vigorous. By the time that the fall is in full swing, your dog will be ready for a long walk in the woods. Besides allowing your pet the opportunity to exercise, this gives you a chance to gaze at the beautiful foliage. This way, both your dog and you can take advantage of all that autumn has to offer.

Daylight Saving

Daylight saving is a mixed blessing. Turning the clock back an hour does give you an extra hour of sleep on a Saturday night in October. And it is lighter in the morning, so the children are safer as they make their way to school. On the other hand, the sun sets an hour earlier. Coupling this with the already shorter days of autumn means your dog finds himself taking his evening strolls in the dark.

You can protect your pet while he is out in the dark by making him more visible. Adding reflective strips to his identification tag, collar and leash can be a big help. You can also purchase collars, leashes and harnesses made of reflective nylon. These items catch the lights from passing cars and help keep your dog from being hit.

Daylight saving time also means new schedules for your pet. While you turned your clock back, your dog did not. His internal time mechanism still thinks that it is an hour later that it really is. So, from his point of view, he is now being fed, exercised and let out at a different time. Since dogs thrive on set schedules, your pet may be confused and anxious.

You can minimize the impact of daylight saving on your dog by making the one-hour adjustment gradually over a few days. For example, if you walked your pet at 6:00 every evening before the time change, your dog thinks that he should go out at 5:00. For the first day, you should walk him at 5:10. On the second, take him out at 5:20. If you push back the departure time by ten minutes a day, his internal clock will be in tune by the end of the week. And then, he will be back on his normal schedule.

Fall Veterinary Care

Autumn is a perfect time to see that your pet's veterinary needs are met. Make sure that your dog is up-to-date on all of his vaccinations, especially if you will be boarding him over the approaching holidays. During the fall and winter, kennels keep their doors and windows shut in an effort to reduce heat loss. This means there is less air exchange with the outside and more air recirculating through the building. As a result, a dog that is boarding has increased exposure to infectious viruses and bacteria floating around the kennel. Current vaccinations help to prevent these infections.

This is also the time to neuter your dog. Youngsters born in the spring have now passed their six-month birthday and are old enough for the surgery. Spaying or altering them now prevents unwanted litters next spring.

Even older pets do well with elective surgery performed in the fall. The cooler weather is easier on the body than the heat of summer. This enables most animals to feel better and heal with less stress. Pets that are kept outdoors no longer have to worry about biting flies that can delay the healing of surgical incisions. So, if you have been putting off elective surgery for your pet, consider getting it done now.

A Change In the Home Environment

With chilly nights here, you will probably turn the heat on in the house. The dropping temperature outside plus the forced hot air inside decrease the humidity in your home. That can create troubles for your dog.

First, his coat may dry out. This reduces its effectiveness as a protector and insulator of the animal's skin and makes him itchy. Another problem is that dry air contributes to respiratory problems such as sinusitis, sore throats and bronchitis. It can also aggravate autumn allergies.

You can add moisture back into your dog's coat by supplementing his diet with essential fatty acids. Dietary supplements can be bought from a pet store or your veterinarian. You can also try using fats and oils readily available at home. Add vegetable oil (like corn oil) and an animal fat (like bacon grease) in a one-to-one ratio to your dog's dinner. Start with a very small amount, such as one-half teaspoon of each. Increase the oils slowly, making sure that the animal does not develop an upset stomach from the additives. Even a large dog does not need more than a tablespoon or two of the mixture. Whether you add a commercial supplement or a homemade one, it takes about six weeks to see results.

The dryness in the air can be alleviated by using humidifiers. You can add a house humidifier to the furnace or place individual humidifiers in various rooms. If you do use a humidifier, however, make sure that it is cleaned routinely. A dirty humidifier can grow molds. The mold spores are aerosolized along with the water droplets and can be inhaled by your dog. This can lead to respiratory infections and allergic reactions. If you cannot clean a humidifier adequately, you are better off without one.

Rodents and Other Pests

As the weather becomes progressively colder, your pet and you will spend more time indoors. Other creatures will also be seeking warm shelters. All too often, they will seek them in your home. You may find that squirrels are getting into your attic and bats are hibernating in the chimney. In all likelihood, rats and mice are moving into any nook and cranny that they can find. If you are like most people, you want these unwelcome guests out of the house.

The best way to stop the infiltration of creatures is to make your home impenetrable. This means putting wire covers over the openings to the attic, chimney and crawl spaces. Also, cover outside stove vents and openings in the foundation with steel wool and wire. This should keep out most wild animals.

However, you may still find that rodents are getting through. The safest way to get rid of them is to have a cat that enjoys hunting. In lieu of that, you may need to use poisons or traps.

Rat and mouse poisons, also known as rodenticides, are very effective, but they can be dangerous for your pet. A dog might eat any form of rat poison, including blocks of bait and trays of grain. He can also be affected by eating dead rats and mice that have been killed by rodenticides. And contrary to popular belief and many product labels, even a small amount of a rodenticide can make a dog very sick.

The symptoms of poisoning in your dog can vary considerably, depending on the type of toxin used. Anticoagulant poisons, such warfarin, cause internal bleeding. Some of the newer products kill the rodents by supplying toxic overdoses of chemicals and vitamins. If your pet ingests either type of rodenticide, he may act lethargic, lose his appetite or vomit. He may also have blood in his stool or urine. There may be bruising of the skin or the whites of the eyes.

It may take several days for the poison to affect your dog. If you suspect your pet has come into contact with a rodenticide or a poisoned rodent, take the animal to your veterinarian immediately. Do not wait until symptoms develop. Your veterinarian may be able to prevent your dog from getting ill. Once your dog shows the symptoms, he is quite sick. He may need to be on medication for several weeks.

When going to the clinic, take the poison package with you, if possible. Different rodenticides require different treatments. If you cannot find the package, bring a sample of the product with you.

Of course, the best way to prevent a problem is to use the rodenticides safely. The tray or bait traps should be placed in spots where your dog cannot go, such as behind heavy furniture and appliances. Or you can put them on shelves and counters that are too high for your pet to reach. Be sure to save the label or package in case of an emergency. You should also immediately dispose of any dead rats or mice that you find around the house.

Another option is to catch rodents using mechanical means, such as traps. You can purchase quick-kill traps at most hardware stores and supermarkets. Using a humane trap allows you to release the live animals after they are caught. Traps are not as neat as poison, but they are safer for the household dog.

Rabies

Your dog may encounter more wildlife during the autumn than in the preceding summer months. At this time of year, wild animals are actively searching for food before the cold weather freezes potential food sources. This increased activity often leads to chance meetings among animals around the neighborhood.

The problem is that wild animals are the main carriers of rabies, a fatal disease that affects the central nervous system. The most common transmitters are raccoons, foxes, skunks and bats.

You should take steps to protect your dog. The best protection is a current rabies vaccination. A dog that has been inoculated against the disease is usually completely protected. This is the reason why most communities have passed laws requiring that all domestic dogs be vaccinated for rabies. If you do not know if your pet's rabies vaccination is current, contact your veterinarian. She has the information on file and can advise you when the next shot is needed.

Another step is to reduce the attractiveness of your yard to wild animals. Most of these foraging animals consider garbage a delicacy. You should pick up any garbage that has been spilled or blown into your yard as soon as possible. Another good idea is to use garbage cans that have tight-sealing lids that cannot be popped open or have special raccoon-proof clasps. By keeping food supplies scarce, you drastically reduce the chance of your dog encountering a rabid animal.

If your vaccinated pet gets into a fight with a wild animal, you still have to act fast. Wash the dog immediately. The rabies virus is carried in saliva. Cleaning an open wound thoroughly with soap and water removes the saliva. Wear gloves to reduce your contact with the saliva while bathing the dog. After the bath, take your pet to your veterinarian for a rabies booster. A current vaccination plus a booster should be sufficient to prevent a rabies infection.

On the other hand, if your pet does not have a rabies vaccination and is bitten by a wild animal, you have a major problem on your hands. A dog can contract rabies and not show symptoms for several months. So, your dog could have the disease and you would not know it. The only way to know for sure is to catch the wild animal and test it for rabies. Otherwise, your pet may need to be quarantined for months. It is possible that he will end up being destroyed.

It is much wiser to play it safe and have your dog vaccinated. You will be doing both him and you a favor.

Thunderstorms

A dog does not have to be caught out in a storm to develop a fear of the rain, lightning and thunder. Even dogs that are bothered by nothing else may find thunderstorms absolutely terrifying. When one hits, your pet may need your help to get through it.

A dog that is afraid of bad weather usually knows when it is approaching. Minutes or even hours before the event, your pet may start to look anxious. He might seek your companionship, hide, tremble and whine. Once the storm hits, an upset dog may just sit on your lap or lie under a bed. But a terrified dog can damage the house and himself. Dogs have been known to tear up flooring, knock over furniture and dig through doors in an attempt to escape the storm.

No animal should be outside during a bad storm. A frightened animal may try to run away. If he gets out of your yard, he can become lost. Even a calm pet can be disoriented and hurt during severe weather. Pets hiding under trees can be hit by lightning or flying debris.

If possible, you should keep your pet with you. Holding your dog on your lap during a storm may be the best solution. You can try diversionary tactics, such as rubbing your dog's belly or playing with a favorite toy. If you cannot comfort your dog or divert his attention, make sure that he is confined in a secure place where he cannot cause any damage. To increase his feeling of security, give him a blanket and a box or crate that he can hide in.

Many owners consider tranquilizing their pets during a squall. This is not a good idea. The problem is that most people give the medication as the storm begins. By the time the drug takes effect, the bad weather has often passed. So, your pet gets hysterical during the storm and then is groggy and sleepy for the next twelve hours. In addition, tranquilizers do not work for every dog. On the other hand, if your dog becomes a terror to your house and himself during storms, you may want to explore this option. You should discuss the matter with your veterinarian before the next event.

Dogs can become accustomed to the noise of storms. You can desensitize your pet by purchasing a recording of a thunderstorm and playing it softly for several days. As the animal gets used to the sounds, gradually increase the volume. If your dog seems nervous at any time, cut the volume back to a level that does not bother him and slowly build it up again. Do not make the mistake of playing it loudly from the beginning. Your pet probably will not adjust; he will become more frightened. It usually takes a few months for an animal to adapt. After that, however, he may be able to get through a storm with no problem at all.

Natural Disasters

Some areas are more prone to natural disasters than others. If you live in one of these, you must be aware that pets are not immune to the dangers. Hurricanes, earthquakes, tornadoes and fires take their toll on pets as well as people. As a matter of fact, a pet may be in worse trouble than his owner; many emergency shelters do not allow pets inside.

You can help your dog by being prepared. Know where you will take your pet if your house becomes uninhabitable. Have provisions ready. Buy a carrier big enough for your dog and keep it stocked. Put in potable water, food, bowls, a can opener, a leash, an extra collar (or harness) and a flashlight. A shelter might let your pet in if you can show that you can take care of him and keep him under control.

In case of fire, plan an escape route for your dog. Figure out how to get him out of the house. Put stickers on the doors and windows that advise firefighters that there is an animal inside. Keep extra leashes in convenient places. In an emergency, your pet will panic. Do not expect him to come when you call or to rest placidly in your arms. You will probably not be able to restrain him without a leash.

And finally, listen to your pet. Dogs have an amazing ability to sense when natural disasters are about to happen. This is why the number of lost pets often increases in the days before an earthquake. It seems that the animals run away and hide from the disturbance if they can. So, if your dog is acting in a very strange manner, listen to the news and look for approaching storms.

Chapter Seventeen
Cool-Weather
Update

Many of the topics covered in the spring and summer sections are not just relevant to the warmer seasons of the year. They also apply to cooler temperatures. While the bulk of the information on the following topics is found elsewhere, there are some important points that you should know about cool weather.

Travelling With Your Dog

While travelling with a dog is never easy, autumn is probably the best time to plan a trip that includes your pet. The pleasant fall weather is more comfortable for him. The car is less likely to become hot and stuffy. If the temperature is low enough, you might even be able to safely leave your dog alone in the car for a few minutes. However, you should still park your car in the shade. While cooler weather means less chance of heatstroke, the sunshine beating on a car window can heat up the interior in a very short period of time. And even if it is cool, your pet still needs adequate ventilation. So, leave the windows open a few inches.

It is easier to find a place to stay with your dog in the fall. Hotels and motels are generally less crowded at this time of year. Since they often need your patronage, they are more likely to allow your pet to room with you. Also, being less crowded, the establishments have fewer clients who might object to animals being on the premises.

However, you should still follow the guidelines put forth in the summer section. Call ahead to find out if your dog will be allowed to check in with you. You should also bring a crate in which to confine your pet. And request that the manager inspect the room with you before you check out.

Travelling by plane is easier in the fall, as well. As stated in the earlier section, the best time to put your dog on a plane is during off-peak hours. This means smaller crowds, less traffic and fewer delays at every juncture of the trip. During the busy summer travel periods, the off-peak times are either very early in the morning or late in the evening. However, the entire period between Labor Day and Thanksgiving is considered off-season. After the children start back to school and before holiday travel begins, there are generally fewer people flying at all hours of the day. This means that you will have more flexibility in choosing a flight.

Besides easier logistics, flying in the fall generally occurs during cooler temperatures. Baggage compartments are usually not as stuffy when it is pleasant outside as they are during hot weather. If your pet has to ride in that section of the plane, he will be more comfortable and safer than in hot weather. He will also be less likely to suffer heat-related problems while being moved from one plane to another at intermediate stops.

Once the holiday season starts, however, you should not take your dog with you on a plane trip. The airports are very crowded at all times of the day; more items are being shipped. Also, bad weather causes frequent delays and missed connections. From the onset of Thanksgiving travel to the end of New Year's Day, the chance of your dog being lost in transit is greater than at any other time of the year. He is better off being left at home.

One last point needs to be made. If you plan to board your dog during the holidays, be sure to make a reservation well in advance at the kennel of your choice. The best boarding facilities fill up fast. The last thing that you need during the frantic holiday season is to be all set for your trip and then find that your pet has no place to go.

Shedding

Dogs shed all year round, but you may notice an increase in the amount of hair falling out of your pet's coat during the autumn. This is the time of year when your dog loses the coarse hair that helped keep him cool during the summer. It is replaced with a new coat of fluffy, finer hair. This will form the dense web that acts as an insulator against the cold.

As discussed in the chapter entitled, "Spring Basics," your dog's changing coat is influenced by the length of the days, not the temperature. So, no matter how warm your Indian Summer may be, the animal will still exchange a summer coat for a winter one. This helps explain why breeds with heavy coats, like huskies, develop thick fur during the fall, regardless of where they live. The composition of the hair in the coat is controlled by heredity; the growth cycle is controlled by the daylight. So, even a dog in Florida will grow a winter coat as the days get shorter.

These finer hairs present a new grooming challenge. While they interlock to form an insulating layer, they can also mat together very easily. Tiny mats will prevent the hair from performing its insulating function. They also pull on the skin and create irritations. The clumped hair can harbor fleas, ticks and other parasites. It also holds moisture and dirt against the animal's skin. This actually chills your dog as the nights turn cooler.

As the new hair comes in, it will need to be groomed on a regular basis to prevent tangles and snarls. Some dogs need brushing every day. When combing your pet's coat, make sure that the comb or brush reaches down to the skin, especially if your dog has a dense undercoat. Besides enabling the coat to function as it should, this will stimulate the skin and help keep your pet clean. If you use a fine-toothed flea comb, you might even pull out any parasites that may have hopped on the animal.

While a fairly large amount of hair loss is normal during the fall, your dog should not have any bare spots. If he does, he should be seen by your veterinarian. Most dogs that are not completely covered by hair have a medical condition that requires diagnosis and treatment. The problem should be taken care of before the weather turns too cold.

Allergies

Allergies can be a problem in the autumn, as well. The cool, damp conditions can make fallen leaves and dead plants moldy. A dog that spends time outside is sure to inhale some of the molds as he plays in the yard and runs through the leaves. If your pet is hypersensitive to the molds, he may develop symptoms such as an itchy face and feet as well as a runny nose and eyes.

Your dog may also have a contact allergy to the dying vegetation. After running through brush or piles of leaves, he can develop red bumps, scabs and scratch marks on his belly, legs or any other part of his body that came in contact with the vegetation. Another sign might be excessive hair loss.

He may try to alleviate his discomfort by rubbing his ears and face along the floor or by licking his feet excessively. And he will scratch himself constantly. As his skin becomes increasingly irritated, there is a risk of infection setting in.

If your dog develops respiratory or skin troubles in the autumn, limit the amount of time that he spends outside. You can also reduce his exposure to allergens by raking up the fallen leaves before they become moldy. Should his symptoms persist or appear serious, the animal should be examined by your veterinarian. Medications such as antihistamines and corticosteriods can help eliminate the effects of an allergic reaction.

Fleas and Other External Parasites

Summertime flea problems will not simply disappear in the fall. If you live in a warm area, these pests will have a field day under the new, dense coat that your dog will be growing. The fine hair creates a warm, undisturbed place for fleas to live and breed. This is especially true if the hair is matted and clumped. Grooming your pet all the way down to the skin will help eliminate the parasites that irritate him and endanger his health.

And if you reside in a cooler climate, do not make the mistake of believing that your flea problem is gone when the first cold night arrives. While fleas prefer the summer, they can actually thrive in the fall. This is due to the damp, humid conditions. The fleas are protected by fallen leaves and decaying vegetable matter; they are warmed by the daytime sun. When it gets cold, the adult fleas do die, but the eggs and larvae merely go dormant. As such, they are alive but inactive. Because eggs and larvae can remain dormant for several months, they can hatch out anytime in the autumn when the conditions are right. Once they do, they will resume the business of hatching, growing, feeding and reproducing.

The indoor fleas and those on your dog will be unaffected by colder temperatures. Both your home and pet will stay warm enough for fleas to complete their life cycle. As a matter of fact, you may be more cognizant of your indoor flea problem. While the adult fleas outside have died, those inside are alive and well.

But autumn is a good time to eliminate fleas and prevent their reappearance until spring. Just like in the spring and summer, you will have to treat your yard, house and pet. Rake up fallen leaves and debris. Vacuum your house thoroughly and throw away the vacuum bag. Then, use the appropriate insecticides in the house, on the yard and on your pet. This will kill the adult fleas and developing larvae everywhere. Meanwhile, the residual insecticide and vacuuming should eliminate eggs and developing larvae in the house. So, your home should be free of fleas. And if the weather stays cold, no new fleas will hatch outside. This means that you will have effectively broken the flea cycle until the following spring.

You need to keep a couple of things in mind when you are eradicating indoor fleas in the fall. First, there is less airflow through your house. Doors are kept shut and storm windows are put up. When using an insecticide, you still need to ventilate the house, even if it is cold outside. To reduce the amount of chemicals circulating throughout your house, you might want to pay more attention to noninsecticidal control. The effectiveness of daily vacuuming can be augmented by sprinkling the carpets and rugs with a desiccant, such as diatomaceous earth or silica powder. This will dry up the fleas. Rather than putting harsh chemicals on your dog, you might try combing him one or twice a day with a flea comb. This will also keep his new winter coat well-groomed and tangle-free.

The second thing to remember is that cold air in the house will not work alone. So, opening all your windows on the first cool day will not stop your flea problem. It might kill some adults. But many adults as well as most of the larvae and eggs will be snug in your carpets and in the nooks and crannies of your home. Even if you bring the interior temperature of the house down to freezing, the eggs and larvae merely go dormant and re-emerge as the house warms back up. Fleas can live several months in sub-optimal conditions and still complete their life cycle in only a few weeks in warm temperatures. Making the house cold for a few hours or days will not end your flea troubles. To break the cycle, you must be more aggressive.

Fleas may not be your only problem in the fall. If ticks are prevalent in your area, they will not disappear with the first cold snap. A hard, deep freeze is needed in order to kill off all of the ticks for the season. And your dog's thicker coat gives the ticks a refuge from the cold. All of that fine, dense hair makes it more difficult for you to find these parasites on your pet. So, continue checking for ticks throughout the fall.

Spiders and insects may stick around for the whole winter. If they live inside your house, they will be unaffected by the outdoor elements. So, you have to keep checking your dog for signs of bites from these pests.

Chapter Eighteen
Home Alone

During the summer months, your dog may have been very fortunate. He may have spent his time surrounded by the children and adults that he loves. However, once the vacations from school and business are over, your family is not at home as much. So, instead of being in a house full of people, your dog finds himself alone for hours on end. And when his family does return, he discovers that everybody is very busy with homework or housework. The animal may end up barely getting a ten-minute walk, let alone the companionship that he craves. Then he might suffer separation anxiety.

Separation Anxiety

Dogs are pack animals. They always prefer to be in the company of other pack members. In the wild, the pack members would be other dogs. In your household, the members are your family and you. If he is separated from the pack for a great deal of time, he will be lonely; he may become very anxious. As a result, he may become destructive.

It is important that you realize that your dog is not misbehaving out of spite or malice. He probably does not even know that he is doing anything wrong. A dog, just like a child, has only a limited number of ways to react to his environment. He uses his mouth and voice to signal distress. So, a lonely, bored dog will find ways to reassure himself and keep himself occupied.

Unfortunately, his activities can be detrimental to both your house and him. He may start chewing on household objects, scratching at doors and clawing at walls. He may also lose his housebreaking skills.

Another possibility is that he may bark incessantly. You may not know that your pet is causing a neighborhood problem because he probably starts barking as soon as you leave and stops when you return. Even though this is not destructive to your house, it can be annoying to your neighbors. You should check with them to see if your dog is causing a problem for people nearby.

Some dogs get so anxious when they are left alone that they literally make themselves sick. They can develop digestive trouble complete with vomiting and diarrhea. Others lick and suck at their skin. This may result in sores that are known as lick granulomas. These are large, raised, ulcerated lesions on the legs.

And the anxiety problems may continue to when you come home. Some pets get so excited when you return that they lose control of their bladders and urinate uncontrollably when you greet them.

Protecting Your Dog and Your House

An anxious dog with time on his paws can get into places that he would never even think of when you are with him. He may develop a sudden liking for the taste and texture of various pieces of furniture, pillows, shoes and clothing. In addition, dogs often find many wonderful things in the kitchen. They have been known to open cabinets and cupboards. There they find all sorts of exciting things that are fun to play with or good to eat. The short list includes foods, packages, cleansers and detergents. There have been cases where a pet has managed to open the medicine chest in the bathroom and eat a large quantity of the pills found there.

Take steps to protect your dog and house from each other. Use child safety latches on cupboards and cabinets. Store poisons and medications out of the reach of the dog. Do not leave your favorite clothing and shoes in reach of your dog's mouth. But not even these steps will give total protection. You may limit the mischief that your dog can get into, but you cannot be sure that everything will be in order when you arrive home.

There is one way to have peace of mind. Consider buying a crate for your dog. A crate does more than just keep your pet from chewing up the house. If properly used, it can make him feel more safe and secure. Canines, by nature, are den animals. They seek the security of a small, closed space to give birth and raise their young. In addition, young canines enter it when they are anxious and need security.

The crate should be large enough for your dog to stand up, turn around and stretch out fully. Put a soft pad or blanket on the floor of the crate; this will help keep your pet comfortable. If you use a woven wire crate, cover the top and three sides with a blanket; this will simulate the interior of a den and give your dog some privacy. He should also have access to water. As a bonus, you might include some food and a few of his favorite toys.

You can reinforce the secure nature of the dwelling by making crate-training a pleasant experience for your dog. The crate should be placed near one of the main areas of activity in your house; this will help keep him from feeling isolated. To get him to go inside, you should put his meals in the crate. Leave the door open the first few times that he eats there. After he has become comfortable with the crate, close the door for brief periods of time. Gradually increase the length of confinement. You should try to get him to go inside when he is sleepy. Soon, your pet will probably seek out the crate on his own when the household becomes too hectic.

When using a crate, you should never confine your dog for longer than three or four hours. A wild canine would not spend all day in his den; you cannot expect your dog to be any different. If you cannot come home at lunch, you might ask a neighbor or friend to stop in during the day and take the animal out to relieve himself and stretch his legs.

Also, it is important that the crate never be used as punishment. Your dog should consider his crate a safe haven. If he thinks of it as a jail, you will create more problems than you solve when you confine him there.

If, for some reason, your dog cannot get acclimated to a crate, you can try confining him to one room in the house. Pick one that gives him plenty of light and air. He should also be able to move about freely. Instead of closing the door, block the entrance with a sturdy child gate. This keeps him in the room while letting him see out. He will feel less caged, reducing his anxiety about confinement.

Some people decide to protect their houses by putting their dogs outside while they are gone. This may not solve your problem because the dog can be just as bored and lonely in the yard as in the house. If this happens, he may start barking and destroying the yard. If he digs under the fence, he may get loose and run away. If you keep your pet in the backyard, he should wear a collar and have proper identification tags. In addition, you should provide him with plenty of fresh water and shelter from the autumn winds and rain.

Solving the Problem

Once you know that your dog and house are safe, you can turn your attention to solving your dog's anxiety problem. It is possible that the root cause is not that he is alone more often; it could be that a physical problem is causing his strange behavior. So, the first step is to take the animal to your veterinarian for a thorough examination. If an illness is the cause, your pet can be treated. If your veterinarian certifies that your dog is in good health, you can concentrate on behavioral modification techniques that may relieve his concern about being alone.

The best way to reduce your dog's anxiety is to minimize the impact of your departure. The goal is to keep your pet from becoming overly excited. Whenever you leave, do make a fuss over the dog. Instead, simply put him in his crate or area of confinement, tell him goodbye and walk out the door. When you come home, be just as calm. This is especially important with a dog that loses bladder control when very excited.

For a couple of weeks or so, you should leave a few times each day for varying lengths of time. Your dog will eventually come to accept your departures and arrivals as normal parts of his routine. And he will know that, even though you go away each day, you always come back. Ideally, this lesson is learned in the summer before the hectic fall schedules begin.

A dog that is left alone also needs a few toys. Leave him rawhide bones and toys that he can gnaw on. This may protect your furniture from unwanted attention during your absence. But do not expect the toys to take your place. Most dogs play with toys only if you are there to stimulate play.

Another idea is to leave on a radio or television. Your pet may be comforted by the music or the sound of a human's voice. Some people even call their dogs on the telephone and leave messages on the answering machines. This gives the animals a chance to hear their owner's voice at various times throughout the day.

Perhaps a neighbor is willing to help. Someone who is retired or not working may welcome the opportunity to visit with your pet for a few minutes each day. A ten-minute walk can do wonders for a lonely dog or neighbor.

If you have a well-fenced yard, you might try putting a dog door on your back door. This gives your dog constant access to the outside, so he does not feel trapped. And you will know that, if you are late from work, he can go outside to relieve himself. Also, if he is outside when an autumn squall hits, he can get to a safe shelter.

While solving a behavior problem, it is a good idea to put your dog through an obedience training course. This will improve the communication between your pet and you. A dog that understands what you are telling him is more likely to obey commands and less likely to act out. The training increases your dog's confidence and helps reduce fear-induced behaviors. And by increasing your understanding of your pet, the training may enable you to find the cause of the behavior problem. Then, you can tailor the solution.

If your dog develops behavior problems that you cannot solve on your own, seek the help of your veterinarian or an animal behavioral specialist. Never tranquilize the dog while you are away. Medication does not cure the problems; it only masks them briefly. In addition, human medicines are not made for dogs. Your dog may become very ill if you administer the wrong type or dose of medication.

Getting Another Pet

From your dog's point of view, having another dog around the house may be the solution to his anxiety problem. It will certainly relieve his loneliness. And it might give him the companionship that he misses when you are gone.

Before you decide to get another pet, consider the pros and cons. Another dog needs attention. The additional food and medical care cost money. A puppy certainly creates new troubles of his own; he needs to adjust to the household and be housebroken. And an older dog may need up to six weeks to adapt to his new family.

On the positive side, another pet may keep your first one happier, healthier and better exercised. A second dog can be another great companion for you. He would add more work, but probably less than you expect. It takes the same amount of time to feed and exercise two dogs as one. And best of all, the two animals can keep each other entertained.

If you are considering a canine addition to the family, take your dog's personality and age into account. In general, younger dogs usually welcome a new friend; adult dogs can adapt well; geriatrics are less tolerant of new arrivals. If you already have a young dog, consider adding a puppy or juvenile dog to the family. That way, his buddy will have about the same energy level. If you have an elderly pet, you may do better to adopt an older, calmer dog as a companion.

Try to pick a breed that complements your pet's temperament. Even the friendliest dogs develop a hierarchy of dominance and submission. One dog will be the boss; the other will be the follower. If the dogs cannot work out a pecking order, they will fight over food, belongings and territory. It is easiest for your present pet if the new arrival is younger or less aggressive. This way, the first dog retains his position in the family.

And avoid putting two unaltered male dogs together. Companion male dogs should be neutered. Two spayed females or a male and a female tend to make better combinations. If you do have male and female dogs, make sure that they are altered to prevent an unwanted litter of puppies.

When you are ready to bring your new pet home, make the initial introduction away from the house and yard. This minimizes any territorial reactions from your dog. Keep the introduction low-key and pleasant. Reassure both animals. You should monitor all of their interactions until they have adjusted to one another. Do not leave the dogs alone until you are positive that they get along well.

Another dog is not your only option. Believe it

or not, a cat can be an excellent companion for a dog. Often a young dog can adapt easily to having a feline for a friend. However, an older dog may not be as amenable to the new addition; he might think that a cat is quarry, not a playmate.

If you think that a feline would be a good second pet, you are better off avoiding a young kitten. Once a cat is twelve to fourteen weeks old, he should be able to take care of himself. Even so, be cautious when introducing the cat to your dog. And just as you would with a new dog, monitor all of their interactions until you are sure that the animals get along.

Chapter Nineteen
Halloween

Halloween is a great holiday for kids and adults who like to act like kids. But Halloween can be a scary and dangerous time for your dog. You should take measures to ensure that Halloween is a safe and enjoyable evening for both your dog and the trick-or-treaters.

Protecting Your Dog

The first thing to remember is that all animals belong inside during Halloween. During Halloween and on the evening before, your neighborhood may be full of mischief makers. Even the nicest kids on the block may be involved in a few pranks. While most of the pranks are meant to be harmless, some get out of hand. Property ends up damaged; people and animals get hurt. A dog that is left outside is an easy target. Even if the dog is behind a fence, he is not safe. Pranksters can jump fences and open gates.

An animal wandering around after dark is in danger. If your dog is not accustomed to being outside, he can easily become lost. Even if he knows the neighborhood fairly well, the bright lights and decorations may confuse and disorient him. Worse still is the fact that your dog is more difficult to spot once the sun goes down. This makes it harder for you to find him if he gets out and more likely that a motorist will not see your dog. It is possible that your dog will be accidently hit by a passing car.

A dog that is loose will encounter other dangers, as well. He can become entangled and hurt by the electrical cords that help light Halloween decorations. He may even try to eat some of the decorations or the remnants of a prank. Ingesting inedible objects, such as those made of paper or plastic, can lead to an intestinal blockage. Items like raw or rotten eggs can cause food poisoning.

Besides internal damage, your dog could experience other problems. Ingesting a bit of pumpkin may not harm your dog, but he could be burned by the candle or shocked by the bulb inside a lighted jack-o'-lantern.

If nothing else, a dog that is out on Halloween will almost certainly come across a group of trick-or-treaters. Their costumes, shrieks and general mayhem may frighten or excite your pet. The running and yelling of little figures in bizarre costumes may elicit a chase-and-nip response in a dog. He may knock a bag of candy from a child's hand and get free-access to the goodies. He can become very sick if he finds a mound of spilled candy and eats all of it.

In addition, you should not send your dog out trick-or-treating with one of your children. A child has to deal with a clumsy costume and a bag of goodies and still watch out for cars on the street. Keeping track of the family dog is an added burden that will be too much to handle. Besides, a costume can restrict your child's range of motion. This diminishes his ability to control the dog. In all of the excitement, your pet may be able get loose and run away. If your child's mobility is limited, he may not be able to stop or catch the animal.

You should do your dog a favor and keep him inside the house both on Halloween and the night before. If he is strictly an outdoor pet, you should let him sleep a night or two in the garage or shed. Anywhere is better than letting him outside. As mentioned earlier, even a barrier such as a fence is really no protection.

You should protect your dog at home, as well. Instruct your children not to share their candy. Nor should you indulge him every time a trick-or-treater rings your doorbell. Too much candy will make any pet very sick. The animal can develop severe stomach aches and intestinal ailments.

And chocolate can be poisonous. It contains a stimulant called theobromine, which is related to caffeine. Too much of this compound causes over stimulation of the gastrointestinal system, which leads to vomiting and diarrhea. It can also lead to nervousness, frequent urination, muscle tremors and a rapid heartbeat. Profound and acute changes to the cardiac and respiratory systems can result in depression and death. Fatalities have been reported from the ingestion of cocoa and chocolate bars.

The sensitivity to theobromine varies with each animal, but even a little milk chocolate can be dangerous. If you do not want your dog to feel left out, give him a few extra dog treats. This will protect him from the unwanted tricks of an overindulged digestive system.

Protecting the Trick-or-Treaters

You should also take steps so that the dog will not harm the trick-or-treaters. Dogs are creatures of habit. In all likelihood, the frequent knocking on the door or ringing of the doorbell will disrupt his normal peace and quiet. And, for an animal as territorial as a dog, the incursion of many strange people into "his" territory can be very upsetting. These alone may be enough to rile your pet. But when you compound the problem by adding boisterous children dressed in unusual costumes, your dog may become very agitated and frightened. In this frantic state, he may react aggressively by jumping on, scratching or even biting the trick-or-treaters.

To help your dog cope, confine him to an area that is far from the hustle and bustle. If more than one adult is in the house, you might ask the additional person to stay with the dog while you answer the door. Or, you could keep your pet in his crate or a quiet, cozy room where he can relax and be safe. Keeping your dog away from the activity will also eliminate the chance that he will dart out when the front door is open. If your pet can remain in a relatively normal environment and with a person with whom he is comfortable, he should be able to get through the evening without any problems.

Costumes For Your Dog

For some people, Halloween is just no fun unless their pet takes part in the festivities. However, you should follow a few precautions and exercise sound judgment when involving your pet in the celebration.

A costume on your pet may be fun for you but probably is not for your dog. The rule is that your dog should wear a costume only if he will accept it with complacent grace and dignity. If your dog resists donning the outfit, you should not force it on him. A pet that is uncomfortable in a costume may hurt himself in a struggle to get out of it. In addition, if you provoke him by forcing the costume on him, he may accidentally hurt you in his struggle to get out of it. To avoid that scenario, you may want to let your dog spend Halloween dressed as himself.

However, if you do put a costume on your dog, you should heed some cautionary advice. You can find appropriate canine costumes at pet stores or in pet catalogs. Buy costumes that are easy to put on and remove. Stick with decorated pet sweaters or ruffles that are easily attached to a standard collar and do not droop over the pet's face. Stay away from masks or hats that will limit your dog's vision. You should also avoid elastic straps or bands that can cut off circulation. The costume should fit comfortably and not restrict normal movement; the animal should be able to eliminate in an appropriate manner. Finally, be sure to keep an eye on your dog while he is dressed up. At his first sign of disgruntlement, take the costume off.

And even if the pet is all dressed up, it is best that he have no place to go. You should not take your dog to a Halloween party. Not all dogs will enjoy a boisterous get-together. There is just too much activity in too small a space. Any dog can rapidly become uncomfortable, scared or anxious. This is especially true when your dog is in an unfamiliar environment. Unless the party is at your house, he should not attend.

Chapter Twenty
Thanksgiving

T hanksgiving is the perfect time to reflect on all the good things in our lives, including our pets. And while you give thanks for your blessings, you can also do a few things for which your dog will thank you.

Avoid Extra Stress

The holidays, often charged with emotions, can be very stressful for animals as well as people. Canines are creatures of habit; they like their lives to be orderly and based on set routines. A large group of people gathered at your house for Thanksgiving may make your dog anxious, especially if the increased commotion is accompanied by a change in his normal schedule of activities. This nervousness will be heightened if many of the guests are rambunctious children or other animals.

If given a choice, most animals will leave a stressful situation. A cat will run away and hide. On the other hand, a dog is more of a social animal. He would rather be in a group than alone. So, if your dog is anxious, he may move out of the main flow of activity but still stay on the periphery. Whether he stays or goes, your pet will probably show his anxiety by acting submissive (crouching, dropping his tail and lowering his ears) or by acting aggressive (raising his hackles, growling and baring his teeth). He may also show a combination of both behaviors.

A child may not understand that the dog would rather be left alone. Many children (and adults, too) do not understand a dog's body language. So, even though the dog has moved to the periphery, the child may continue to pester the animal until he overreacts and responds aggressively.

You should take a few steps to protect the dog and children from each other. First, it is a good idea to introduce each child to the dog. Make introductions in a quiet, controlled manner. Put the dog on a leash and allow him to settle down. Once he is relaxed and comfortable, you can let the children meet him. They should approach one at a time, being friendly but quiet. Each child should slowly offer the back of the hand without making any sudden, jerky motions. If the dog stays relaxed, the child may pet the animal and the introductions can continue. If the dog shows signs of anxiety or becomes upset, you should break off the introductions and separate the pet from the children. However, if the dog remains friendly, he might enjoy meeting everybody.

Once the introductions are completed, tell the children not to bother the animal. Explain that the dog will approach them if he wants their attention or if he wants to play. However, you should never let a child play with your dog unless the two of them are well-acquainted. Even if your pet is extremely friendly, you should supervise their romping to stave off any accidents.

The best thing that you can do for your dog when your home is filled with activity is to have a place where he can get away. You may also find yourself confronted with a situation where you need to separate your dog from the other guests. You should set aside a quiet, cozy place where your dog can escape from the ruckus. You may want to move his crate or kennel to a room that is out of the way. Or you can simply let him have the entire room to himself.

You need to remember a few things when confining your dog. First, if you must remove your dog from the activities, you should not make a big show of doing so. Quietly take him to his special place and instruct the children to leave him alone while he is there. Next, you should make sure that he has plenty of water. You should also try to maintain his normal schedule. When it is time for your dog to eat, you can feed him in his room. Be sure to check on him periodically.

And most importantly, you should not confine your dog in a crate or a room for more than a few hours at a time. A dog will be content in his crate for three or four hours, but not all day. Dogs and wolves share an instinct for using small places like a cave, den or crate as a home. However, a canine in the wild would not be comfortable spending a great deal of time there without going out. You cannot expect your dog to behave differently.

One last point should be made about confining your dog. If one of your guests brings a dog, that animal should stay with his owner or have a separate place of confinement. Placing two dogs unfamiliar with each other in the same room is begging for trouble. If one or both should feel nervous or threatened, you may have a full-scale dog fight on your hands.

Do Not Overfeed Your Dog

We are all familiar with the effects of overeating at Thanksgiving. Often, instead of feeling thankful at the end of the meal, we feel stuffed and uncomfortable. Just because you splurge at a Thanksgiving feast does not mean that your dog should, too. All that extra food will not make your pet love you more. In fact, it can have a disastrous result; your dog can become very sick.

If your dog overeats, he may experience mild dietary upset. If you are lucky, the condition will disappear after a few uncomfortable days. However, it is possible that your pet will develop a serious condition known as bloat. It can be caused by your dog eating large amounts of foods to which he is not accustomed. His stomach can fill with gas and expand. The expanded stomach may actually rise and twist on itself. This traps food in the stomach and results in the loss of normal blood circulation to the organ. Dogs with bloat suffer from severe metabolic complications that require immediate veterinary care. It is much safer for your pet to stick with his own diet.

Another possibility is that your dog may develop pancreatitis. The pancreas is the organ that secretes enzymes which help digest food. If it is overtaxed by too much fatty food, it can oversecrete digestive fluids. The excessive enzymes damage the pancreas's cells and leak into the surrounding tissues.

There they can "digest" organs and body fat. This leads to more inflammation and illness. In some cases, the dog can be poisoned by his own digestive system.

The symptoms often include loss of appetite, severe vomiting, diarrhea and dehydration. Also, the animal is unable to digest additional food. Dogs with pancreatitis often have to be hospitalized for several days to receive adequate treatment and fluid replacement. The condition can be fatal. Animals with mild cases usually recover, but the illness often recurs. Once the pancreas has been inflamed and damaged, it is likely to malfunction again.

Even if your dog does not get sick from overeating, the extra fat and sugar-filled treats add unnecessary calories. These extra calories add up rapidly and will increase your dog's body fat and weight. This is especially true if your pet is older or not getting enough exercise.

You should plan ahead to keep your dog from being overfed during Thanksgiving. Give him his normal meal about an hour before the feast begins. This way, your pet will be less likely to act hungry. Without a deprived look on the animal's face, the sympathetic family members may avoid overindulging him with scraps. If you cannot control the guests, however, you may have to put the dog in his crate or a separate room during dinner.

If you just cannot keep the food and your pet separated, be very cautious about what he eats. You should not give him bones from a turkey or any other poultry. They are hollow and very brittle; they splinter easily. These splintered pieces are very sharp and can perforate a dog's intestines or cause an obstruction. These conditions can require surgery to treat and may be life-threatening.

Instead, feed him only plain turkey without skin or bones. This minimizes the fat and indigestible materials that can lead to trouble. You can also allow him to eat cooked vegetables or raw carrots. Better still, give your dog a few extra dog treats. This will prevent a guilty conscience from haunting you the entire day.

But by far, the best thing that you can do for your pet on Thanksgiving is to give him some special attention. An extra walk, extra game of fetch or simply keeping him on his normal schedule will mean more to your pet than food. By substituting these for fatty tablescraps, you will be doing your dog a real favor. And he will thank you for it.

Part IV

Winter

Chapter Twenty-One
Winter Basics

Just thinking of winter conjures up visions of snowball fights, sled rides, and romps in the snow with the dog. It is also a time to keep warm and protect ourselves from the cold. We wear heavier clothes; we also winterize our cars and our houses. Your dog needs to prepare for winter, as well. Even though he has a fur coat, he must adapt to the new season or he will have trouble coping with the cold. And just like people, pets that get cold can suffer ill effects.

A dog that is primarily an indoor animal should not have too much trouble in the winter. He can wear a coat and boots for protection when he is outside. When he is inside, he will not be subjected to the elements. On the other hand, a dog that spends the bulk of his time outdoors will be exposed to the dangers of the cold weather. You can minimize the risks by helping your dog make needed adjustments to the rigors of winter.

Water In the Winter

Just as in the summer, the most important thing that you can do during the winter months is provide your dog with constant access to clean, fresh water. Animals that are exercising or working are as likely to suffer from dehydration in the winter as in the summer. This is for two reasons. First, their owners often do not supply enough water. Many people link dehydration with heatstroke; they mistakenly believe that water is a hot-weather issue only. This erroneous conclusion frequently leads to a lax effort in keeping the dog's water dish adequately supplied. All animals need water every day of their lives in order for their bodies to function properly. Regardless of the temperature, a lack of water will result in dehydration.

The second reason many dogs suffer dehydration in the winter is that the water in a dog's dish can freeze rapidly. Ice is an inadequate source of water. First of all, most dogs chew ice only when they are hot; they do not lick it when they are cold. Second, the dog may not be able to break the ice in his water bowl into edible-size chunks. Snow is not beneficial, either. Even if ice and snow worked as substitutes for water, a dog is not be able to consume enough to meet his needs. Water must be in its liquid form to quench a dog's thirst and replenish his body fluids.

To help your dog avoid dehydration when it is bitterly cold outside, you must bring him fresh water several times a day. That will not work, however, if you are away for several hours at a time. In order to keep the water from freezing, you may have to purchase a special heater for your dog's dish. And avoid metal water bowls. A dog's tongue can stick to a steel bowl if the temperature is freezing.

Winter Shelter

Even though your dog has a fur coat, you cannot leave him outside unprotected during the winter.

Even dogs bred for cold-weather climates need shelter. We have all seen movies where huskies in Alaska survive being exposed to temperature extremes. The reason these dogs make it through raging blizzards is that they know instinctively to make a depression in the snow, curl up and then let the snowfall cover them. In effect, this creates a small den that blocks the wind and is warmed by the dog's body heat.

While your dog's coat may help keep him warm, he still needs to have protection from the wind, rain and snow. A domesticated dog has not been bred for the same jobs as a working husky. He may lack the ability to create his own den. You have to provide your dog with adequate shelter. Without it, your pet can suffer from frostbite and possibly freeze to death.

Proper shelter means a structure that allows your dog to be warm, dry, out of drafts and off the damp ground. The best shelter, of course, is your own house. But if your dog is left outside for any length of time, he should have a doghouse.

You can find doghouses at pet stores, hardware stores and even lumberyards. Or you can build one yourself. They come in a variety of sizes, shapes and materials. The traditional doghouse is made of wood with a shingled, sloping roof and an open front. It looks nice in the yard but has several drawbacks. The opening does not block drafts. Wood is a poor insulator and attracts insects; it is also difficult to clean.

Newer houses are made of plastic resins and other materials that are good insulators and easy to clean. A house made of plastic or foam may not blend into the landscape as nicely as a wood house, but it will be a better home for your dog.

When selecting or building a house for your dog, size is the critical issue. Just like the den the huskies create in the snow, the structure is warmed by the body heat of its occupant. If the house is too large, the dog is not able to generate enough heat to keep the house and himself warm. In this case, smaller is definitely better. A house that is the proper size has just enough room inside for the dog to turn around and lie down comfortably.

The shelter should be positioned so that the interior is not subject to drafts. The entrance can be angled away from the prevailing wind. Place a flap over it to help block drafts. Another possibility is to install a partition just inside the door; this will create a separate area from where the dog enters the house and where he lies down.

The house should be raised off the ground a few inches; you can set it on bricks or blocks. This keeps moisture from seeping in through the floor. But the house should not elevated to the extent that the dog has difficulty getting in and out.

A good doghouse does not need elaborate furnishings. All that is required is some sort of bedding. Regardless of what type you provide, the bedding should be easily removed. It needs to be cleaned or replaced often. Dirty bedding contributes to parasite infestations and skin problems. Straw is often a popular choice for bedding. However, it is a favorite domicile for parasites and insects. And once straw is matted down, it loses its insulating properties. A better choice is a clean, dry blanket or towel. Remember that the prime generator of heat to keep the animal warm is the dog himself. The bedding provides insulation and makes the dog more comfortable.

Cold-Weather Feeding

As the outside temperature falls, your dog's body will lose more heat to the environment. So, he will use more energy to keep his body at its normal temperature during the cold winter months. It takes additional calories to meet this increased demand. That usually means your dog will need more food.

It is a mistake to think that all dogs should eat more just because it is cold outside. If your dog is a house pet, he does not need additional food to compensate for the few extra calories that he expends on his daily walks. Adding calories to his diet will probably make him fat.

But if your dog is a working animal or spends most of his time outside, you may notice that he acts hungry and starts to lose weight. Since his coat alone does not keep him warm, he needs to maintain a healthy level of fat and muscle. You can help him do this by raising the amount of calories that he consumes. Depending on the breed and his work load, he may need anywhere from a 10 to 50 percent increase over his summer diet.

There are two ways to add calories. The first is to simply increase the amount of food that the dog eats daily. Feed him more at each meal or increase the number of meals each day. Another variation is to leave dry food down all the time and hope that he eats as much as he needs. This will not work, however, if your pet's energy demands are too great; he literally will not have a large enough appetite to eat enough dry food over the day. So, while a sedentary outside pet that usually eats once a day may do fine with two meals daily, a hunting dog that works and lives outside may lose weight, even if he eats "free choice" all the time.

The second option is to increase the amount of calories in each bite of food. This is usually done by adding meat or fat to the ration. This raises the caloric content and has the additional benefit of increasing the diet's palatability, so that the dog wants to consume more food. If you add meat, it should comprise approximately 10 to 15 percent of the total diet. If you are using fat or grease as an additive, add only a very small amount. This allows you to make sure that your dog tolerates the extra fat without getting digestive upsets or diarrhea. If he does fine, the amount of grease can be increased slowly until it is approximately 3 percent of the diet. If you do not want to add extra fats or meat, you might consider changing your dog's normal food to one designed for dogs with high-energy demands. These are very calorie-dense, highly-palatable foods.

It is important to realize that your goal is to provide your dog with enough food to keep himself warm. It is not to make the animal fat. You should strive to keep your dog's weight constant all year round. If he maintains his proper weight during the winter months, he does not need extra calories. If you notice that your dog is losing weight during cold weather, add more calories to his diet. If he starts to gain weight, cut back. And if you do increase the amount of his winter provisions, be sure to adjust it back down when spring arrives.

Winter Illnesses

Both people and dogs seem to be sick more in the winter than at any other time of year. When it is cold outside, most structures are sealed up to keep the warmth in. Windows and doors are closed and insulated with weather stripping or by storm windows and doors. While the cold is kept out, the amount of air exchange is restricted, as well. With less air flowing in and out of a house or office, viral particles can become concentrated. This increases the exposure of both animals and people to these infectious agents. In turn, it also increases the number of sick people in close contact with each other.

In addition, people and animals contract illnesses more often in the winter because the immune system seems to work less efficiently. Less time is spent outdoors getting exercise and sunshine. As a result, the body is not as strong as it might be in other seasons. This may affect the body's ability to fight off a virus.

Pets and people do not commonly share the same illnesses. While there are some diseases that can be transmitted back and forth between your dog and you, most are species-specific. This is especially true of viruses. Viruses that attack dogs are very contagious to other dogs, but not to humans. So, you may have the flu and your dog may be sneezing and coughing. But you can console yourself with the fact that you did not give the illness to your pet. Rest assured that he did not transmit it to you, either.

Strep throat is another wintertime illness that your family probably did not get from your dog. This sore throat with fever is caused by bacteria that are very contagious among people. While it is true that a dog can carry strep bacteria, he does not bring them into the house. Instead, he is infected by a human family member. The bacteria then lives in the dog for a few weeks before dying out on their own. If your family seems to suffer from bouts of strep throat all winter, your veterinarian may suggest putting your dog on antibiotics. That way, if someone has infected your pet, he will not be able to give it back to anyone else in the family.

If your dog is actually sick, you should take him to your veterinarian. An animal illness is often harder to treat than one in a person. Viral and bacterial infections in dogs often affect the respiratory, digestive and nervous systems. Treatment may involve medications and fluids available only at your veterinary clinic.

Treating a sick animal at home is difficult. You cannot force your pet to eat, drink or spend the day resting in bed. You may be tempted to treat him with over-the-counter medications designed to relieve similar symptoms in people. While some human medications can be beneficial, none should be used without consulting your veterinarian first. Obviously, the physiological make-up of a canine is very different from that of a human. So, the types of medication and doses used for dogs are different from those for people.

For example, the dose of aspirin that is effective for a person is detrimental to a dog. The drug may cause ulcers and stomach upsets that can lead to internal bleeding and vomiting. Your veterinarian can give you the necessary guidelines for medicating your dog. As a rule, however, it is not a good idea to give aspirin to your dog routinely.

While you cannot force your dog to eat, you can take a few steps to encourage him. Feeding small amounts by hand may entice him. Warming his meals to just a little above room temperature often helps. And chicken soup may be as good for a canine as it is for a person; the fats, flavoring and aroma may entice him to eat. In addition, baby food is good; it is a highly palatable source of protein. Try warming chicken or turkey baby food and mixing it with a small amount of your dog's regular fare, or with bland foods such as white rice and cottage cheese.

Playing In Snow or On Ice

Just because your dog has four legs does not mean that he is better equipped than you for playing outside in the cold. He runs the same risks that you do. In fact, he may have more trouble; he cannot wear boots with treads and he has no traction if snow clumps between his toes. He can easily slip and fall when walking or running on snow or ice. And the results can be the same. Your dog can suffer sprains and strains of ligaments, tendons and muscles. He can also have broken bones. You should take the same precautions when playing outside with your dog as you would if playing with a child.

In addition, you should be especially cautious when playing or walking near a frozen lake, river or pond. Dogs do not know instinctively when the ice is too thin to hold them. If the ice cannot support your weight, then your dog should not be on it either. Also, do not let your dog venture too close to the edge of the ice. He may accidentally slide off into the water and be pulled under the ice by the current. An animal that loves to swim may even jump in. Your dog does not always have the sense to be careful; you have to be responsible for his safety.

The Young and the Old

One last bit of advice needs to be given regarding basic winter activities. Children and older people are more susceptible to the dangers of winter. They are less able to maintain their body weight and caloric intake. They are also more likely to be injured or freeze than a healthy adult.

Dogs are no different. If you have a puppy or an older dog, take extra precautions in the winter. Make sure that this special pet is kept warm, dry and well-fed. A youngster may love the cold and snow, but he can easily get chilled. Do not leave him out alone. Limit outside playtime to brief periods during the warmer, well-lit times of the day. An older pet's body may be bothered by the cold and damp. Do not push him to exercise. Brief walks to keep joints lubricated are all that he needs. And when inside, he should have a pad or blanket to lie on; this will keep him off of the cold floor.

Chapter Twenty-Two
Winter Dangers

The winter poses many dangers for your dog. While the cold is the prime source of problems, it is not the only one. Other elements combine with cold temperatures to create deadly predicaments. In addition, many of the products used to fight the effects of the cold have dangers of their own.

Wind and Water

In almost every weather report, the absolute temperature is not the significant reading. The true measure is one that factors in the wind chill. This is the effect of the wind on the temperature. The low temperature for a particular day may not be uncomfortable. By itself, it might be invigorating. But when a strong breeze is added, the low reading can plummet to dangerous depths.

The wind affects a dog just like it does a human; wind rushing across the animal draws heat away from his body. Most dogs are better-equipped to handle the effects of wind than their owners are. A canine's entire body, including the extremities (the head, paws and tail), is covered with hair; this reduces the speed at which heat escapes. But heat loss at a slower rate is still heat loss. Over time, the body will suffer the effects of being chilled.

The amount of time that a dog can be exposed

safely to the cold is detemined by his age and body mass. A thin puppy will lose heat more rapidly than a mature, healthy dog. A large Mastiff is better able to withstand the cold than a tiny Chihauhau.

The length and density of the dog's coat is also a factor. The hair in the coat creates a tightly woven and dense covering that resists airflow and acts as an insulator. It reflects heat generated by the body back onto the dog and keeps cold air out. Some dogs are more suited for the cold than others. A dog with a fluffy coat generally has a thick undercoat that adds protection. Other dogs have only a smooth, short-haired coat to fight off the cold. This is not a good insulator, so those dogs are more likely to chill.

If a dog is wet, the dangerous effects of the cold and wind increase significantly. When the hair gets wet, it lies flat. As a result, the coat loses its insulating properties and the protective layer between the dog and the environment disappears. The wind is able to blow through the coat and chill the body faster. Dogs with heavy undercoats are still protected if their outer coats are the only ones that get wet. They still have the undercoat to insulate the body. But if both coats are wet, a dog will chill.

Besides diminishing the insulating effect of the coat, water has another harmful consequence. As it evaporates, water pulls heat away from the body. This exacerbates the reduction in body temperature.

You have to take steps to reduce the effects of wind and water. First, you must provide adequate shelter. As discussed in the chapter entitled "Winter Basics," a doghouse that blocks the wind, is up off of the ground and equipped with a blanket or towel will provide a place for your dog to stay warm outside. On bitterly cold days, however, your dog should be inside your house. This is especially critical for older dogs and those with joint problems, such as arthritis.

Another step is to groom your dog regularly. Frequent brushing keeps the hair of the coat from matting. To be effective, the hairs need to lie next to each other. Matted hair tangles up; a coat that is full of knots cannot insulate a dog from the cold.

If your dog gets wet from playing out in the snow or rain, you should dry him off with a towel. For a dog with a thick coat, removing as much water as possible from the top coat may keep the undercoat from becoming wet. A dog with a short coat will be wet all the way through. Towelling him off not only reduces the amount of water on the animal, it also massages and stimulates muscles and joints that may have stiffened in the cold. And it has an added benefit; most dogs enjoy the invigorating massage.

If it is raining or there is snow on the ground when you go out with your dog, you might put a towel in the dryer just before you leave. By the time you get back, it will be nice and warm. Your dog will certainly appreciate that.

Hypothermia

If your dog gets too cold, he may suffer from hypothermia. Hypothermia is the medical term for a body temperature that is below normal. This condition occurs when a dog gets too cold and his body cannot generate enough heat to maintain its normal internal temperature. As the temperature falls, the animal's internal organs and systems cease to function properly. Hypothermia can be fatal.

Dogs that are wet and cold are prime candidates for hypothermia. So are dogs that cannot regulate their body temperature accurately. These include puppies, older dogs and dogs that are underweight, sick or injured. Puppies have a large body surface relative to their weight and do not yet have a fully-developed adult coat. This results in a large area for heat to escape from. In addition, a very young puppy cannot shiver, which is the body's reflexive way of generating heat. Older, thin or infirm dogs often have less body mass than younger and healthier dogs. They do not have any body stores from which to draw calories to generate heat. Also, a dog that is old or unhealthy may have a coat in poor condition.

You should be able to easily determine whether your dog has developed hypothermia. As the condition starts, he will shiver violently and be cold to the touch. He will also be very lethargic. If the hypothermia progresses, you might notice that his pupils are fixed and dilated and that his respiratory rate and pulse are very low. He may lose his ability to shiver. If not treated, he could lapse into a coma and die.

You will have to act rapidly if your dog develops hypothermia. Warm the dog by placing hot water bottles or a heating pad around his body. If the animal is wet, rinse him off with warm water and then dry him thoroughly. You can also use a hair dryer set on low to help dry and warm the animal.

Even though you need to act quickly, the dog should be warmed up slowly. A hypothermic dog burns easily. Applying heat directly to the animal's skin may lead to a loss of fluids across the burned area. The skin may not regenerate and there is a strong possibility of infection setting in. If it becomes generalized throughout the body, the infection could threaten your pet's life. So, burning your dog in your rush to help him will assuredly complicate his predicament. And while the skin is being scorched, the body temperature can still be dangerously low.

Do not place the hot water bottles or heating pad directly on the dog. Wrap them in a blanket or towel. If he is lying on a heating pad, you should turn the animal periodically. This aids in circulation and prevents the portion of his body on the heating pad from overheating. If you use a hair dryer, keep it on its lowest setting. Test the hair dryer on your own skin; the air should not feel too hot or burn you.

After you started to warm your dog up, wrap him in a towel or blanket and take him directly to your veterinarian. Once you are at the clinic, your doctor can implement and supervise a warming process that gives your pet the best chance of a full recovery.

Frostbite

Frostbite occurs when tissue becomes so cold that it is damaged. The extensive chilling results in a lack of circulation to the area. The decreased blood supply deprives tissue of oxygen and vital nutrients. If not stopped, frostbite causes tissue destruction.

The extremities, such as the ears, tail and feet, are most susceptible to frostbite. When it is cold outside, the circulation to these areas is limited to reduce heat exchange with the environment and keep the body core warmer. Also, in many cases, the extremities have less hair that other parts of the body. This increases their exposure to the cold. The feet are especially at risk. Frozen mud, snow or ice can become packed between the toes, providing a direct source of cold that contributes to frostbite.

If your dog develops frostbite, the affected area will initially turn white and whatever hair is there may fall out. As it thaws out, the tissue swells and becomes red. It is also extremely painful.

If you think that your pet is suffering from frostbite, warm the area and take the animal to your veterinarian. Just as with treating hypothermia, the goal is to bring the temperature back to normal gradually. Wet heat is generally better than dry heat. But the water in the hot water bottle should not be too hot. You do not want to shock or burn your dog. In addition, you should not vigorously rub the frostbitten area. The circulation in the area will not be good; you could easily damage the overlying skin.

Once your dog arrives at the clinic, your veterinarian can warm the affected area safely and monitor your pet's progress. The veterinarian can determine if the normal blood supply is returning and put your pet on antibiotics to help control any infection.

Recovery depends on the extent of chilling. If the area is only mildly affected, your dog may recover fully. However, many frostbitten areas do not return to normal. Some extremities do not regrow hair. Others have regrowth of hair, but it may be white. Freezing may have destroyed the pigment in the superficial skin layers. However, if the area has been severely damaged, there may be no return of circulation. In a case such as that, the frostbitten toe, ear or tail may have to be amputated.

Preventing Hypothermia and Frostbite

You can take steps to diminish the chances of your dog suffering either hypothermia or frostbite. First, you should limit the animal's time outdoors in extremely cold weather. A general rule is that if it is too cold for you to be outside, it is probably too cold for your dog.

Whenever your dog does go out into the cold, you should determine whether he needs added protection. A dog with short or coarse hair probably needs a coat. His hair is not enough insulation. A short-haired dog does not have an undercoat; a coarse-haired coat allows too much air to circulate on the body. In addition, an indoor dog that goes outdoors only fifteen minutes a day needs more protection than a dog that is outdoors most of the time and adapted to the cold.

Many people think that it is silly for a dog to wear a coat. However, it is not. Many animals that spend a lot of time indoors wear coats when outside. Consider horses. Most of them wear blankets and coats during cold weather. No one casts disparaging looks at them. The same should apply to your dog.

Coats for your dog can be purchased at most pet stores and through catalogs. If you decide to use one, be sure to buy a coat that is easy to put on. Many coats fasten easily around the dog's chest. However, coats that go over your pet's head are often hard to use. Your dog may resist your efforts to put the wrap on him. If you have to wrestle your dog every time that he is going outside, you will probably not use the coat as often as you should.

On the other hand, a long-haired dog should not wear a coat. His hair does an excellent job of insulating the skin and keeping the dog warm. Putting a coat on would flatten the hair and cause it to mat. Once this happens, the hair loses much of its ability to protect the dog.

A sweater provides additional benefits. Besides keeping your dog warm, a sweater protects the animal's underside from road salt and irritating chemicals. Even though a sweater is not recommended for keeping a long-haired dog warm, it can help if your neighborhood has a lot of salt and chemicals on the streets and sidewalks. Whether you use a coat or a sweater, be sure to launder it frequently. This will keep the garment clean and remove substances that could irritate your dog's skin.

Paw Problems

A dog's paws are sensitive to winter's hazards. Frequently, they can be soaked by water and covered by mud. If his feet stay wet and filthy, the result can be tiny cuts and cracked pads, which can cause lameness. The moisture and dirt also create the perfect environment for the overgrowth of bacteria and fungi. This can lead to skin infections developing between the toes and spreading up under the nails.

In addition, snow or mud can cling to the hair on the paws and actually force the toes apart. This prevents the dog from walking correctly and impairs circulation. In severe cases, packed snow and mud can lead to frostbite.

Also, consider the effects of road salt. Every winter, the roads and sidewalks get a liberal coating of salt to melt the ice. And every winter, you see the corrosive damage that the salt does to cars. It can also cause damage to your pet's feet.

Road salt is very irritating to the skin. When your dog walks on a salt-covered road or sidewalk, or even in plowed-up snow, he runs the risk of embedding some of the granules in his paws. As the salt rubs against the pads, it can make the feet raw as well as set the stage for blisters and infection. At the very least, your pet will end up with very sore paws. The salt can also burn the dog's belly if he kicks it up on himself when running. To compound the problem, the animal will probably try to rid himself of the salt by licking his feet and abdomen. He may ingest a few of the granules. This can cause mouth irritations and stomach upsets.

In addition to the road salt, you should beware of other substances used to make driving and walking safer. The chemical compounds often used on roads and sidewalks can burn your dog's skin or cause internal problems if swallowed. The sand often mixed in with the chemicals is very abrasive. It can get caught in your dog's hair and rub the skin raw, creating the possibility of infection.

If your dog experiences minor foot irritation, you may be able to aid healing by rinsing and drying his feet after he comes inside from a walk. If the problem is severe, you should take the animal to your veterinarian. Topical medication may be used to treat and soothe the skin. If there is any infection, your dog may need systemic medication.

In most cases, however, you should be able to prevent the sore feet, mouth and stomach associated with wintertime walking. When you are out with your dog, you should stay on the sidewalk but let the animal walk in the snow. This allows you to take advantage of traction that the salt, sand and chemicals offer while reducing the chance of your dog irritating his feet. When you return home, you should rinse and wipe off his paws. And use a towel to wipe off his chest and underside. This will remove any traces of irritants picked up when he crossed a sidewalk or street covered with chemicals. And you should clean out any packed snow that might be between the toes.

Another solution is get your dog a pair of boots. They will shield his feet from wintertime snow, ice, salt and chemicals, and also protect them from hazardous road materials, such as broken glass and loose gravel. Since boots keep his feet dry, they will help prevent sores, infection and frostbite. When wearing boots, your dog may have an awkward gait for awhile. But he will get used to them.

Dogs with long hair will also benefit from boots. Snow and ice often catch on the hair on the legs. As the snow and ice build up, they start to clump together with the hair. This can prevent your dog from walking in a normal fashion. In addition, the clumps pull on your dog's hair; this irritates the skin. Then, as the snow melts, the moisture will create an ideal environment for bacterial overgrowth and skin infections. A pair of boots prevents this from happening.

If your long-haired pet refuses to wear boots, you might clip his paw hair to a moderate length. This facilitates snow removal and the cleaning of his feet. The hair should not be shorn completely, however. It does protect the feet from the cold, snow and other winter hazards.

Winter Burns

There are times when winter can be too hot for your dog. Veterinarians see more burn injuries on animals during the winter than at any other time of the year. This is because we use supplemental heat sources during cold weather. You may augment your heating system with portable heaters. Or you might enjoy a fire in the fireplace every so often. Your dog is bound to investigate the unfamiliar sights and sounds. In the process, he may stick his nose and paws in places where they should not go.

Pets can get burned from a variety of other sources. One is the soothing wintertime beverages. Any hot liquid that is swallowed by or spilled on your dog can result in a painful burn. Even sleeping too long on an electric blanket can build up an excess amount of heat under your dog's body and lead to a burn.

Fireplaces cause a number of accidents. Young animals may burn themselves because they do not know enough to stay out of a fire. In addition, sparks often pop out of the fireplace as the wood burns down. A dog warming himself or sleeping in front of the fire may be burned if a cinder lands on him. Putting a screen in front of the fireplace keeps your dog from getting into the flames as well as prevents cinders from flying out.

The worst burns come from portable electric heaters. As with a fireplace or a wood stove, your pet may fall asleep too close to the heat source and burn himself. In addition, the cords to these heaters are usually exposed; many animals chew on them. The result can be a nasty electrical shock and severe mouth burns. Another danger is that many heaters can be easily knocked over by an animal. If that happens, the heater will pose a fire hazard for the entire household. You should never leave your dog alone in a house when a portable heater is on.

If your pet suffers an accidental burn, treat him in the same way that you would treat a person. Put ice on the burned area immediately. Then seek proper medical care; take the animal to your veterinarian. The damage caused by a burn can be deceptive. Only your veterinarian can determine what the proper treatment should be.

Antifreeze Poisoning

The last wintertime danger is antifreeze. This product works wonders for your car, but it can be disastrous for your pets. Antifreeze is very toxic. Unfortunately, it has a sweet scent and taste that attracts animals. They will lap up antifreeze spilled on the driveway or road, or lick it off of their feet if they walk through it. The ingestion of a very small quantity may be fatal for your dog. It has been documented that as little as a teaspoon of antifreeze can kill a cat.

Pets that accidently drink antifreeze suffer irreversible damage to their kidneys. If untreated, they become very ill within twenty-four hours and can die within two days. These pets exhibit vomiting and depression; they can slip into a coma.

If you think that your dog has swallowed antifreeze, do not wait for him to show signs of illness. Take him to your veterinarian immediately. Your doctor can test for poisoning and start treatment before the poison takes effect. Once the antifreeze has started to damage your pet's internal organs, the treatment is much less effective. The danger cannot be overemphasized. Even with proper care, many animals do not survive antifreeze poisoning.

Rather than risk this kind of disaster, you should exercise prudent measures when working with antifreeze. When you drain your radiator, put the used liquid in a sealable container. As you replace the fluid, avoid spilling any of the liquid onto the garage floor or the driveway. If you do spill some, clean it up immediately. When the job is finished, dispose of the empty containers and the used antifreeze, following the manufacturer's instructions. And keep any unused portion sealed tightly in its original container, out of reach of your pet.

Chapter Twenty-Three
Christmas

Christmas is one of the most joyous times of the year. Even if you do not observe Christmas, you probably celebrate a cheery, wintertime holiday. Friends and families get together. The house is decorated inside and out. Everyone always seems to be in a good mood. With proper planning, the good spirits can last the entire holiday period.

Holiday Decorations

Keep your pet in mind as you decorate your house. Decorations go up once a year and for a brief period of time. Your dog will be interested in the new and unusual objects scattered around the house. He learns by pawing, biting and chewing. If you do not take steps to prevent problems, your dog may learn the hard way that the object he is investigating can be harmful. At the same time, the decorations need to be protected from your dog.

The first item to be concerned about is the focal point of all decorations, the Christmas tree. Decide whether to put up a live or artificial tree. If you are like most people, the effect on the dog will not be the prime criterion for selecting your tree. But there are some things that you should be aware of.

The trunk of a live tree is often coated with fertilizer and insecticide. And when the tree is placed in a stand and watered, the chemicals on the trunk contaminate the water. If your dog drinks it, he may become sick.

Also, the needles begin to fall out as the tree ages and dries. Although these needles are not poisonous, they are very sharp. They can penetrate the skin and cause abscesses. If your dog tries to eat them, the needles can cut his tongue, lips and gums. If swallowed, they are relatively indigestible and can actually pierce the lining of the stomach and intestines.

On the other hand, artificial trees are made of synthetic material. They do not require water and their needles are not dropped. However, their branches can be pulled out easily. The artificial needles are often sharp and always non-digestible. If your dog were to chew one of the branches, he would probably ingest many of the needles. Just like the needles from a live tree, they can cause gastrointestinal problems, such as bleeding and blockage.

You should use your own experience with your pet when deciding on what type of tree to get. If your dog drinks only from his water bowl or you have a tree stand whose water well is inaccessible, you may want to get a live tree. If you do not want to vacuum up needles every day or your dog must drink any water he finds, you are probably better off with an artificial tree. But if your dog leaves new objects alone, you can probably pick either type of tree.

Once the tree has been selected, you must decide where to place it. The ideal location is in a room that can be sealed off from the dog. If you can close a door to the room whenever you cannot supervise your pet, you will not have to worry about the tree being damaged or your dog getting hurt. However, most people want their trees displayed prominently. These trees are readily accessible to their pets. If a curious dog knocks over a decorated tree, you may have a horrible mess of tangled branches and broken ornaments.

You can have your tree in the center of the living room and still protect it from the exploits of a rambunctious canine. But you have to take some additional steps when setting it up. One of the best measures is to secure the tree to an adjacent wall or to the ceiling. This can be done by tying some sturdy line to a couple of points on the tree and fixing the line to nearby walls. You should have at least two lines, each running to a different wall. Or you could use one line from the tree to the ceiling. Fishing line is good to use; it is very strong and nearly transparent. It will not detract from the beauty of the decorated tree.

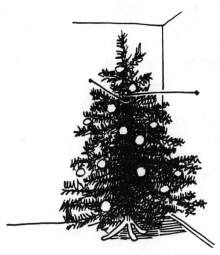

If no line is available or the tree is too far away from a wall to make tying it down practical, you can try some other methods of keeping the dog at bay. You can place the tree behind a barrier. Child gates, playpens or Plexiglass screens will work. The barrier should be easy to erect and dismantle. You probably will not want it up when guests are over or other times when your family is enjoying the tree. If the barrier is too much of a hassle, you will not use it.

If protecting the tree is going to be an annual event, you may want to take the time to create a barrier that adds to the holiday decor. Then, you will not have to dismantle it every time company comes over. A short picket fence can be painted in festive colors or have drawings sketched on the slats. Be as creative and elaborate as you want.

After you are certain that the tree is safe, you should turn your attention to the decorations that go on it. The lights pose a couple of dangers. First, they get very hot after being on for awhile. They can burn your dog if he touches them. When you put the lights on the tree, you might want to keep the last string at a height that the dog cannot reach. If you want lights all over the tree, you should place the lower lights away from the tips of the branches. Your dog will have a more difficult time reaching them if you attach them to the inner portion of the branches.

You should also make sure that your dog cannot reach the electrical cord that runs from the lights to an outlet. Your pet can be electrocuted if he chews on the it. The cord should be folded up and tied with a twist-tie or rubber bands. String or tape can secure the cord in a position that is inaccessible to your pet. Also, you can purchase a special box to cover the excess electrical wiring and switches; these boxes often resemble a wrapped present, so they will not detract from the festive environment. And to be on the safe side, you should leave the lights unplugged unless you are in the room.

You also need to be concerned about the ornaments. Avoid using glass ornaments. These are usually extremely fragile and break easily. The shattered pieces are very sharp. They can cut your dog's mouth and feet. If any of the pieces are swallowed, the glass can puncture the intestines, which can lead to peritonitis and possibly death. The ornament hooks are also very sharp. They, too, can be picked up and swallowed, resulting in digestive tract troubles such as obstructions and punctures.

Store-bought decorations made of gingerbread

and cookie dough should also be avoided. You should not purchase strings of foodstuff such as popcorn or cranberries, either. These items are not really edible. They contain powerful preservatives and hardening agents, and are often painted. If your dog eats them, he may be poisoned.

If you make your own homemade edible ornaments, do not put toxic agents in them or paint them. The only problem with edible ornaments is that your dog may try to eat them. A hungry dog may knock or pull a tree over in his quest for a string of homemade popcorn or a gingerbread Santa. You are better off avoiding edible ornaments whose aroma may entice your pet to misbehave.

The safest Christmas ornaments are those that are one-piece and made of a nonbreakable, nontoxic material. They should be too big to swallow. In addition, hang them above the reach of a curious canine's mouth and paws.

One of the most dangerous materials put on Christmas trees is tinsel. Animals are attracted by its bright finish and flexibility. If your dog tries to eat some, there is a good chance that the tinsel will become wrapped around his tongue. As a pet struggles to remove it, the tinsel is often stretched out and becomes wrapped even tighter. It can cut the sensitive tissue in the mouth and stop the circulation of blood to the tongue. If a strand of tinsel is swallowed, it can bunch up and block the intestines. The sharp pieces can also cut through the intestinal walls. Dogs that swallow tinsel usually require surgery to remove it. The prudent course is not to put any tinsel on your tree. You lose the icicle effect, but your dog is much safer.

And keep in mind your dog's safety as you decorate other parts of the house. Lit candles can burn a curious pet. They can also be knocked over and start a fire. Food packages wrapped as gifts and left under the tree can entice a hungry animal. The result can be torn-up presents and a dog with a stomach ache. Icicles and tinsel draped on mantles are as dangerous as tinsel on a tree. And centerpieces of dangling streamers and feathery fronds are simply irresistible to a curious pet.

Holiday Plants

Besides a decorated tree, many houses are adorned with other greenery. Holiday plants add a festive touch. However, many have an ominous aspect as well; they are poisonous.

Mistletoe contains chemicals that stimulate the muscles lining the digestive tract, resulting in nausea, diarrhea and other signs of gastrointestinal upset. Severe cases may result in dehydration as well as elevated blood pressure, pulse and respiratory rates. It can be fatal.

The poinsettia plant is another potential source of trouble. Although opinions vary, most veterinarians feel that the plant is dangerous for your dog. The plant produces a milky sap that is released as a dog chews on the leaves and stems. If your pet swallows the plant's leaves, he can end up with inflamed gums, tongue and intestines. Also, the sap will irritate his eyes and skin if it gets on the dog's face.

Holly, Jerusalem cherry, amaryllis and the bulbs of most plants are also toxic. Their ingestion leads to symptoms such as digestive upset, frothing at the mouth, crying, depression and muscle twitching.

If you see your dog eat a toxic plant or if he displays any of the signs of being poisoned, you should take him to your veterinarian. For most of the plants, there are no antidotes. However, the doctor can treat the symptoms until the effects of the poisons wear off.

It is easy to protect your dog from poisonous holiday plants. The obvious method is to place the plants in spots inaccessible to your dog. If the animal cannot reach the plants, he cannot be poisoned by them. Another idea is to use artificial plants. Unlike a few years ago, today's synthetic plants closely resemble real ones. You often cannot tell the difference. And should your dog decide to examine them, he will not be poisoned.

Holiday Stress

The holidays are joyous, but they can also be stressful. Last-minute shopping, cooking extravaganzas and the invasion of friends and family can frazzle even the most even-tempered person. All of the frantic activity will be stressful for your pet, as well.

Dogs are creatures of habit. They need time to adapt to any changes that take place in their environment. For your dog, the holidays have a profound effect. The decorations change the physical nature of his domain. He will notice the frenetic behavior of the other members of his family. And if a guest brings a pet of his own, your dog will have territorial and compatibility issues to deal with. Any one of these would be mildly upsetting on its own. However, when they occur collectively, they can turn your pet into one anxious canine.

The stress that a dog feels at Christmas may be more severe than at Thanksgiving. The difference is that the disruptions of Christmas usually last for two or three weeks while Thanksgiving lasts just a day or two. Because the time period is longer, your dog is more likely to exhibit behavioral changes. His anxiety may lead him to do things that he has not done since he was a puppy. He may begin to chew on objects and to eliminate in the house. He may also become more aggressive. Some dogs get so stressed that they make themselves physically sick, often with episodes of vomiting and diarrhea. That, in turn, increases their anxiety. They can end up hurting themselves or someone else.

You need to help your dog get through the holidays. You should strive to maintain the dog's normal schedule. He should be fed and walked at the same time every day. His diet should not be altered. And just as at Thanksgiving, your dog should have a special place where he can retreat. This can be a crate or an entire room. During the holidays, you should not disturb the make-up of that area or room; it should not be decorated. The point is to give your pet a place that remains normal amidst the chaos.

Presents For Your Dog

Our dogs are part of our families. As you shop for family and friends, you may find yourself searching for the the perfect gift for your dog, as well. If you do, you will not have any difficulty finding a present. Just about every pet, novelty and department store has suitable gifts for the well-loved canine. But there are some guidelines that you need to follow.

The prime consideration is safety. Any toy for your dog should be selected carefully. Do not purchase an item that can be easily broken or chewed apart. Your dog may swallow some of the pieces. This can lead to perforated or blocked intestines. Should this happen, your pet will most likely spend the holidays in the hospital.

Among the many good toys are nylon toys and bones made for dogs. Hard rubber toys that are too big to swallow are also great choices. If you want to get your dog a flying disk, purchase one made especially for dogs. These are usually stronger than those made for humans. The latter tear apart too easily.

Dog treats are good gifts, too. You can purchase many varieties of dog treats, but there are a few human treats that are not good for a canine. Do not give your dog chocolate. It is poisonous to a dog and will make him sick. However, you might be able to find some "chocolate-covered" dog treats. These are made with a substitute that looks and tastes similar to chocolate but is safe for dogs.

Alcohol is also toxic. Small amounts of a drink like eggnog can make a dog disoriented and ill. Too much can lead to liver and heart disease. It can be fatal for a puppy.

Unless your pet has a bad stomach, most animals can handle an occasional treat from the holiday dinner table. Avoid feeding your dog fatty pieces; they often cause stomach upset and diarrhea. Instead, give him scraps of lean turkey, beef or lamb. He may also like some vegetables and rice. If you do feed your pet tablescraps, be careful not to overindulge him. The added calories are a present that your dog should have only in moderation.

Dogs love bones, but they are a treat to be given cautiously. The bones must be strong enough to withstand the pressure of a dog's gnawing. Poultry bones are too brittle; they will splinter and can be swallowed. They can get caught in the throat or the intestines. A better choice is a large knuckle bone or marrow bone that has been boiled. But even these can have pieces that break off and be swallowed. So, keep an eye on your dog while he chews his bone. If the bone looks like it is going to break up, you must take it away from your pet. Even if it does not splinter, there is the risk of your dog breaking a tooth while he chews.

Rawhide bones and products are great gifts and safer than real bones. Rawhide does not splinter and will not cause a broken tooth. Most dogs love the taste of rawhide. And it is digestible. In addition, a rawhide chew helps remove tartar from the teeth and near the gumline. Avoid giving your pet too much rawhide at one time, however. If he swallows large pieces without chewing them, he can get an upset stomach.

If you want to get really creative, you can make your own dog treats. Buy a cookie cutter from a pet store in the shape of a bone or another dog treat and create your own wholesome dog snacks. You can usually find recipes attached to the cutter or in canine magazines. These treats contain no artificial flavors or colors and have no preservatives, so they are good for your pet. In fact, because they are made with natural ingredients and are so good, you may have to keep the rest of your family out of the dog's cookie jar! And just like any other treat, be sure to limit how many your dog is given at any one time.

Although we usually think of edible treats or chewable toys as presents for our dogs, there are many other gifts for pets. Think about orthopedic pads for older, stiff dogs. You can buy special cushions, waterbeds, and heated pads for dogs to sleep on that keep them off the cold floor and soothe tired joints. You can also get elevated stands for tall dogs, so their food bowls are easier to reach. Or, you can buy your favorite pet a new sweater, rug, boots, collar or anything else that you can think of. The list is truly endless and limited only by your imagination.

Even though you can be as elaborate as you want, a very simple gift will please your dog the most. What he wants for Christmas is the same thing that everybody else wants: love and companionship. An extra dose of both will be the best present that he gets.

Giving Dogs as Presents

Pets make great gifts. They are warm and

friendly; they bring companionship to their owners. And giving a pet provides that animal with a much-needed home. But you must follow one crucial rule: never make your gift a surprise.

You must discuss your gift with the recipient in advance. You may think that a cuddly puppy under the Christmas tree is the perfect present. But the person who is going to be responsible for the animal may have other ideas. Many people are not ready for a pet, especially without prior notice. Even though you have good intentions, the dog may end up as an unwelcome animal.

There are two ways to handle a "pet present." One is to tell the recipient in advance and allow him or her to pick out a pet before Christmas. Then, the dog can arrive in time for the holidays.

The other way is keep the gift idea a secret until Christmas. You can announce your present by putting a gift certificate from a shelter or breeder under the tree. Or you can wrap up a collar, toy or some other item that a dog needs. Include a note, saying that at the recipient's convenience, you will take him or her out to get a dog. Then, the prospective owner can pick out his or her new companion. Everybody should have the opportunity to chose their own pet.

Involving Your Dog in the Holidays

Your dog does not have to stay on the periphery during the holidays; he can get involved. Many people love animals but cannot own them. Either they are not capable of caring for them or they live in an environment that prohibits pets.

A visit from your dog might make them very happy and bring some much needed companionship. Many local humane societies have a "Pets To People" or a "Pets On Wheels" program. They will teach your pet and you how to go into homes and hospitals to cheer the residents. These programs bring all types of animals into facilities such as nursing homes and the children's wards in hospitals.

However, you should not simply wander into a health care facility. You should go only with an organized group. You can check your area to see which organizations sponsor this sort of activity.

With a program such as this, everybody wins. The patients enjoy meeting and petting the animals. The dogs love the extra attention. And you get the satisfaction of spreading some holiday cheer.

New Year's Resolutions

As the new year draws near, you will be making resolutions for yourself. At the same time, you might want to make a few promises to your dog. Some suggestions are listed below.

- Spend more time playing with your pet
- Increase the amount of exercise
- Participate in an obedience class
- Solve any behavioral problems
- Be more compassionate regarding your dog's needs
- Groom your dog on a regular basis.

- Feed him a balanced diet.
- Take the animal to the veterinarian for a complete physical examination
- Keep all of your pet's vaccinations current

If you keep these promises, your dog will be healthier. Without a doubt, both of you will be happier. And together, your pet and you will enjoy the new year and the many seasons to follow.

Index

Pecos Press presents....

Becoming Best Friends

Building a Loving Relationship Between
Your Pet and Your Child

by Jane E. Leon, D.V.M. & Lisa D. Horowitz

Even the most gentle animal may become aggressive after the arrival of a new family member. **Becoming Best Friends** teaches you how to prepare your pet for a new baby as well as protect your child from being endangered. With this book, you can turn a potential problem into a nurturing relationship of love and trust.

Among the topics covered are:

- Getting your pet used to a child BEFORE your baby arrives
- Solidifying the relationship as your child grows
- Recognizing danger signs
- What to do if a problem develops
- Animal diseases that may affect your child

170 pages $8.95   ISBN 0-9625043-2-7

Available in bookstores everywhere!